englandsnorthwest

Published by The Bluecoat Press, Liverpool
Book design by March Design, Liverpool
Book production Compass Press Ltd.

ISBN 1 872568 95 5

PHOTOGRAPHY

Front cover: The Lowry (picturesofmanchester.com/Len Grant).

Back cover: Bassenthwaite (NWDA).

The principal photography is by Bill Meadows.

We wish to thank the following companies and individuals for supplying additional photographs:
AstraZeneca, Avecia, BAE SYSTEMS, Bentley Motors, BNFL, British Waterways, Granada Television,
Lancashire County Council, Liverpool Daily Post and Echo, Manchester Evening News, Marketing
Manchester, Northwest Development Agency, Oldham MBC, Rheged, Royal Exchange Theatre, Trafford Park
Heritage Centre, United Utilities, Urban Splash, John Calderbank, George Coupe, Len Grant, Alex Laing,
Angela Mounsey, Ron White and Colin Wilkinson.

englandsnorthwest is published The Bluecoat Press in association with the North
West Business Leadership Team and the Northwest Development Agency.

The North West Business Leadership Team is a group of prominent business
leaders from Cheshire, Cumbria, Greater Manchester, Lancashire and Merseyside,
committed to the long-term well-being of North West England and all its citizens.
The Team was launched in 1989 by HRH The Prince of Wales, and has been at
the forefront of the region's strategic economic development since that date.

For further information, visit www.nwblt.co.uk

The Northwest Development Agency (NWDA) was established by the Government
in 1999 to drive forward the economic development of England's North West. As an
advocate for the region, the Agency with its many partners, leads the development of
the regional strategy which will deliver sustainable economic growth and prosperity
through physical and social regeneration and support for business, ensuring that all
the people of the North West benefit from an improved quality of life.

For further information visit www.nwda.co.uk or www.englandsnorthwest.com

englandsnorthwest

The Bluecoat Press

Geographically, the North West is a region of sharply contrasting features, which range from the densely populated conurbations of Merseyside and Greater Manchester, to the unspoiled rural areas of Cumbria and the North Pennines.

Three National Parks – the Lake District, the Peak District and the Yorkshire Dales – contribute to the region's physical splendour. These were established in the 1950s to conserve their scenic landscapes. Of the three, only the Lake District lies wholly within the North West region. This is renowned for its glaciated lakes and also contains England's highest peaks – Scafell Pike, Helvellyn and Skiddaw.

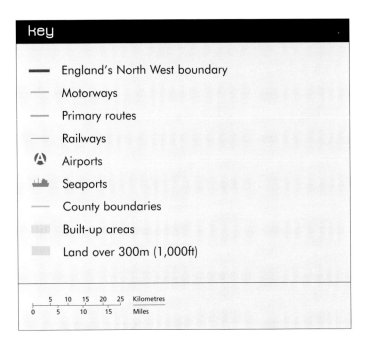

key

━━	England's North West boundary
───	Motorways
───	Primary routes
───	Railways
Ⓐ	Airports
⛴	Seaports
───	County boundaries
▓	Built-up areas
▓	Land over 300m (1,000ft)

Kilometres					
0	5	10	15	20	25
0		5	10		15 Miles

4

contents

england's north west
a region reborn

Trevor Bates

'Boldness. And again boldness and always boldness.' Danton

For such a relatively small corner of the globe, England's North West has tended to exert a disproportionately powerful influence on the way modern society goes about its daily life. Industrialisation, free trade, the co-operative and suffragette movements and life-changing advances in transport, science and medicine, all have their origins in the region. Its bright ideas have been the currency of progress.

This legacy of resourcefulness, expanding the frontiers of knowledge and social betterment, nurtured over three centuries, continues to drive its nearly seven million citizens along new paths of endeavour and achievement.

The pioneering spirit of the Victorians and their forebears has many contemporary echoes. Take industry; the mechanical processes developed by the textile innovators Samuel Crompton, James Hargreaves and Richard Arkwright, gave momentum to the Industrial Revolution. Their ingenuity has been matched in the last half century by gifted people like the aeronautical engineer Roy Chadwick, by Sir Alistair Pilkington, originator of the famous float glass process, and by Anand Dutta, Barry Furr and Frank Hutchinson, whose work on developing the AstraZeneca cancer drug Tamoxifen has prolonged the lives of hundreds of thousands of women.

Science, too, has provided its latter-day icons in the dedication of Sir Bernard Lovell to radio astronomy and Tom Kilburn and Freddie Williams' work in developing the stored-memory computer, the engine of the Information Technology revolution.

The lineage of talent is equally apparent in the cultural arena, but whereas William Wordsworth and Beatrix Potter captivated their fans with poetry and prose, the Beatles wowed the world with classic rock. If there is such a thing as native genius, 'englandsnorthwest', as the image builders now like to brand it, has it in rich measure.

Time and again the region has displayed a remarkable capacity for thinking the unthinkable and changing the way the world lives and works. Communications are another case in point. The canal system, the passenger railway, the inland port and the first motorway, all derive their parentage from the Mersey corridor, or the Red Rose county of Lancashire.

Opposite The stark beauty of the Lake District, looking across Ullswater towards Patterdale.

Above Bowness-on-Windermere. Tourism is essential to the Cumbrian economy and the controls of the National Park and local authorities have managed to preserve the delicate balance between the attractions of the natural landscape and the demands of visitors.

Opposite The Lake District is the most written about and visited area of its kind in Britain. Millions flock here each year to enjoy the extraordinary variety of green pastures, wild fells, beautiful lakes, stately buildings and picturesque villages and towns.

This ambition, to be always in the vanguard of innovation, finds expression today in the continued success of the widely acclaimed Metrolink tram system, in the growth of Manchester International Airport as a global hub of air travel and in the way that Liverpool John Lennon Airport has furthered the cause of low-cost travel to Europe's premier cities.

But the North West is much more than a laboratory of change. It is a region richly endowed with majestic landscapes and seascapes, vibrant cities, historic towns, world-class heritage, a huge variety of tourist attractions, great sporting prowess and an industrious population, cosmopolitan in its make-up and outlook.

Over the last century the region has become a standard bearer for cultural and ethnic diversity, settling successive waves of Irish, Jewish, Caribbean, Pakistani, Bangladeshi, Indian and Chinese immigrants. Their enterprise is plain for all to see in the trading emporiums and restaurants of Manchester's 'Curry Mile' and in the Chinatowns of the region's two great cities. Many of their offspring are now represented in the mainstream activities of regional life – business, the professions, service industries, construction, sport and entertainment.

England's North West enters the third millennium with much greater confidence about its future. Billions of pounds are being invested in regenerating its towns and cities, expanding its educational, sporting and leisure facilities and modernising its business base, transport infrastructure and utilities.

In recent years the gradual onset of regional government and the establishment of a partnership culture have stimulated a growing sense of regional identity and coherence. Civic insularity is giving way to shared pride in the North West's diverse strengths, assets and attractions. With Manchester hosting the 2002 Commonwealth Games in the year of the Queen's Golden Jubilee, this is an appropriate time to reflect on, and celebrate in words and images, what makes this region so distinctive.

Some of our team of writers are native born, others migrated into the region to work and have become adoptive North Westerners. Yet we are all united in the belief that the region possesses special qualities. We have tried not to dwell too much on the region's illustrious past, but as Sir Bob Scott reminds us, 'you cannot understand the present and construct the future without understanding the past'.

Although some parts of the landscape still bear the scars of two and a half centuries of industrialisation, great strides have been made in restoring the physical environment. For example, over £3 billion is being invested between 2000 and 2005 in making good and modernising the water and waste water infrastructure.

Above One of many great country houses throughout the North West, Hoghton Tower can boast two important guests. For almost a year, a young William Shakespeare lived here, during one of the formative periods of his early life. In the Great Hall, James I sat down to a gargantuan three day feast, during which his admiration for a particular piece of beef moved him to knight the joint, 'Sir Loin'.

Opposite The waterway link between the River Weaver and the Trent and Mersey Canal has been reopened after major restoration work on the 1875 Anderton Boat Lift, an important piece of mid-Cheshire's industrial heritage which has been described as 'the Eiffel Tower of the waterways'. The King's Division Normandy Band added pomp and circumstance to the celebratory opening by playing 'Rule Britannia' as the first boat began its ascent.

Thirty of the region's 34 beaches have reached the required EU standard – the highest number yet recorded. Rivers flowing into the Mersey Basin are the cleanest they have been since the Industrial Revolution. Dolphins have been sighted in the Mersey Estuary and salmon have reached as far inland as the River Bollin.

In landscape terms, the region has inspired poets, writers and artists for generations. It is, as Robert Waterhouse notes, a region 'of infinite variety' – fertile plains, high fells, moorland, increasing forest cover, shimmering lakes, national parks and an extensive coastline.

Heritage is another great defining characteristic of a regional identity and Greater Manchester, Merseyside, Cheshire, Lancashire and Cumbria, the five interlocking blocks of this geographical jigsaw, can all lay claim to noble architecture, splendid feats of Victorian engineering, fine cathedrals, great country homes and a treasure-house of galleries and museums. But this is not a region trapped in time. The trading exchanges, warehouses, cotton mills and docklands which generated Britain's wealth in the nineteenth and twentieth centuries, have been reincarnated as hotels, designer fashion outlets, trendy apartments, leisure palaces, or as spawning grounds for the new digital media industries of the twenty-first century.

13

14

Liverpool's majestic waterfront and Manchester's imaginative re-use of its 'cottonopolis' heritage bear striking testimony to this flourishing renaissance. 'A great city to be young in' is how Sir Bob Scott describes Manchester in his thoughtful, comparative essay on the region's two major cities. 'Manchester has muscle and ambition,' he observes, 'Liverpool reputation and potential'. Together they represent 'the raw material of a world-class region'. Civic leaders of both cities took a similar view in 2001 when they signed a formal concordat pledging co-operation in the wider interests of their respective cities and the region.

More often than not the real essence of a region is to be found in its smaller towns and cities. Here, the North West provides a rich tapestry of architecture, tradition, industriousness and local pride. Former mill towns like Blackburn, Macclesfield and Oldham contrast sharply with the historic visitor appeal of Lancaster, Chester and Nantwich.

Changes in the way people work and play are forcing some of our best-known towns to reassess their business profile in the twenty-first century. Relaxation of the gaming laws could pave the way for Blackpool to become a Las Vegas-type casino resort. Warrington on the other hand seeks recognition as a home for knowledge-based industries. Market towns, too, are keen to exploit their potential as enterprise and service hubs as part of the radical restructuring of agriculture following the 2001 foot and mouth outbreak.

Above The family grave of Ellen Nutter, an alleged witch. Pendle became infamous in 1612 because of its association with witchcraft. Today, such a reputation has been turned to its advantage, giving it a unique tourist appeal that is enhanced by the sombre mass of Pendle Hill.

Opposite Clitheroe is typical of North West towns, full of history and charm. The town charter was granted in 1147, making it the oldest in Lancashire. The Norman castle offers a panoramic view of the town and Pendle Hill beyond.

16

The belief in 'getting on' runs deep in the North West psyche, submits Peter Elson in his chapter on the region's attractive and diverse townscape. This virtue was clearly evident when seven local towns sought elevation to city status as part of the Golden Jubilee celebrations. England's only honour went to Preston, the county town of Lancashire which has grown in stature as an administrative and retail centre and a modern seat of learning.

Of course, it is people, not places, that give a region its dynamism. In this respect, too, the North West has an enviable list of great achievers. English Heritage's Blue Plaques Scheme for Merseyside is an instructive guide to the calibre of inventors, pioneers and social visionaries this region has produced: Sir Ronald Ross (malaria pioneer), Sir Henry Tate (art benefactor), William and Eleanor Rathbone (social reformers), Wilfred Owen (war poet), Captain Noel Chavasse (double VC hero) and in more recent times, Beatle John Lennon.

Above The world famous Liverpool skyline. The long-standing rivalry between the two great regional cities ensures a constant search for improvement and progress.

Opposite Manchester captured in the last sunlight of the day. A regional financial, business and cultural centre, it is undergoing a renaissance which is redefining the whole concept of urban living.

Above *Although shipping traffic in the upper reaches of the Manchester Ship Canal is now less than in its heyday, the waterway remains navigable right into the heart of Trafford Park. The new Centenary Bridge, which was opened in 1994 to coincide with celebrations to mark the canal's centenary, allows ocean-going vessels to make regular deliveries of cargo into the world's first purpose-built industrial estate.*

Opposite *Jodrell Bank radio telescope, the brainchild of Sir Bernard Lovell, reinforced the region's reputation for scientific innovation. World attention was focused on the unique telescope in 1957 when it tracked Sputnik 1, the first satellite to be launched into the Earth's orbit. The Lovell Telescope is being rebuilt for the second time to probe ever deeper into the universe.*

Manchester, which runs its own such programme, has erected over 50 commemorative plaques to famous people whose lives touched the city in some way. Richard Cobden (free trade pioneer), Emmeline Pankhurst (founder of the suffragette movement), John Dalton and Ernest Rutherford (scientists), Frederick Henry Royce (of Rolls Royce), William Temple (Archbishop of Canterbury) and Dr Chaim Weizmann (first President of Israel) are but a few of those honoured.

The roll-call of notable sons and daughters from other parts of the region is equally distinguished. Industrial innovators, philanthropists, politicians, artists, entertainers, writers, poets, aviators and sportsmen have all left their mark on the region, the nation, and the world. In his chapter on the great and the good, Martin Wainwright reflects that 'each achiever has thrived in a context which encourages dogged persistence and hard work.'

Who will carry the torch for the late twentieth and early twenty-first century? The Beatles, Sir Chris Bonington (climber), Lord Melvyn Bragg (arts broadcaster and writer), Sir Bernard Lovell (astronomer), Tom Bloxham (urban developer), Robert Powell and Ben Kingsley (actors), David Beckham and Michael Owen (footballers) and Sir Alex Ferguson (football manager), represent rich seams of talent and seem obvious candidates for a contemporary hall of fame.

19

Above The Open Golf Championship at Royal Birkdale, Southport. The North West possesses some of the finest golf courses in the world and Birkdale, Hoylake and Lytham are all internationally known for hosting The Open.

There will be many others as the region capitalises on the rich promise of its ten universities, expanding science base and twenty-first century industries. Bioscience is a case in point. Genomics, tissue engineering, biomedical implants, drug discovery and bioinformatics – areas where the North West has a growing track record – all offer considerable scope for entrepreneurial exploitation.

Information and communication technologies are generating an equally exciting future as befits the region's status as the cradle of the computer industry. The fusion of IT skills with the creative industries has led to over 70 per cent of all Japanese computer games being written in the North West. Virtual Reality, perhaps the next great computing innovation, is being developed locally to levels that will continue the region's commercial advantage for many years to come.

The marriage of knowledge and enterprise is sparking investment in new facilities like the University of Liverpool's £23m Biosciences Centre, Lancaster University's Infolab project and UMIST's new Information Technology Venture Centre (IT-VC). At Daresbury Laboratory in Cheshire, home of the world's first synchrotron light source, a new science park is being built

to transfer research into the market-place. The x-ray light source was used to reveal the structure of the foot and mouth disease virus and most recently to discover how our bodies produce energy, an area of science which won the Cambridge scientist Sir John Walker part share in the 1997 Nobel Chemistry Prize.

The region's inventive instincts run deep in its business base. Companies – large and small – are pace-setters in many fields. United Utilities is helping the government meet its green energy targets by setting up a not-for-profit company to champion renewable energy technology; Pilkington has delivered yet another first with a glass that cleans itself; and British Nuclear Fuels carries its advanced nuclear technology across the world, from USA to Japan.

Lever Fabergé's two sites at Port Sunlight in Warrington and Wirral are home to well known brands like Persil, Domestos, Surf and Comfort, products which can be found in nine out of ten UK homes. A great deal has changed since William Hesketh Lever built the world's largest soapworks in 1888, but innovation is still the key to success. Half of the products made at Port Sunlight today were not manufactured on the site five years ago.

Above The North West is the birthplace of rock climbing. Early Victorian pioneers honed their skills on the crags of the Lake District and then took their nascent skills to the Alps and further afield. The tradition continues with many of today's great climbers, such as Sir Chris Bonington, acknowledging their debt to the challenges of the fells.

Right Manchester International Airport, with a recently opened second runway and a new rail link, now handles over 19 million passengers a year, 85 per cent of whom fly to international destinations.

Right below Liverpool John Lennon Airport was the fastest growing European airport in 2001. An impressive new terminal building is a promising sign of the airport's aspirations and confidence in the future.

Many companies are finding that progress and social responsibility are not mutually exclusive. The Co-operative Bank, an integral part of the UK's Co-operative sector, has pioneered internet banking alongside an ethical policy which dictates who it will and will not do business with.

But it is not all work. The leisure revolution is transforming the way people enjoy their playtime. Here, too, England's North West is building a formidable record of cultural, tourism and sporting excellence. Visitors can take their pick from a vast range of indoor and outdoor recreational pursuits, whether it be rock-climbing, horse-racing, visiting bird sanctuaries, concert-going, viewing dramatic performances, gallery-hopping, designer shopping or night-clubbing.

The two newest attractions, Michael Wilford's award-winning Lowry and Daniel Libeskind's Imperial War Museum North, on opposite banks of the Manchester Ship Canal, are striking examples of the region's ability to build a future of rich promise on the legacies of the past.

Up and down the region, from the Beacon in Whitehaven to Wigan Pier and Liverpool's Maritime Museum, the great cultural and tourism potential of a reinvented past has already been aptly demonstrated. As our final contributor Felicity Goodey makes clear, a whole new era of cultural, creative and economic opportunity now beckons for 'englandsnorthwest'. The architects of today's renaissance tread ever more confidently in the footsteps of their pioneering predecessors.

Above The M6, incorporating the Preston bypass, Britain's first motorway, runs as a spine from north to south and is bisected by motorways linking all the major conurbations.

23

a landscape for all seasons

Robert Waterhouse

'A thing of beauty is a joy for ever:
its loveliness increases; it will never pass into nothingness.' John Keats

England's North West is a region of quality landscape of almost infinite variety. From High Peak moor to Cumbrian fell, via bucolic Cheshire and the market gardens of Lancashire – not to mention an extensive coastline connecting Wales with Scotland and a 120-mile Pennine range to the east – the North West has it all.

Conservation of national parks, designated areas of outstanding natural beauty and sites of special scientific interest ensure that, by and large, this landscape is protected, maintained and equipped to receive its annual millions of visitors.

If the Lake District is the most celebrated, and most visited area, there are good reasons. The coincidence of high fells – three peaks over 3,000ft – and long, deep, freshwater lakes is unique in Britain, a sort of Alps in miniature though of course very different in feel. The closeness of the West Cumbria coast, the Solway Firth to the north and Morecambe Bay to the south gives the Lakes a sense of apartness belied by the M6 motorway and the London-Glasgow railway line just to the east.

The Lake District has a national park all of its own. To its south east, Cumbria and Lancashire slice into the Yorkshire Dales National Park. At the other end of the region, parts of Cheshire form the north west segment of the Peak Park, a lung of moorland and forest between Manchester and Sheffield. These are less dramatic but still substantial hiker hills, liable to sudden changes of weather even in summer.

The view westwards from Shutlingsloe on a fine day stretches right across the Cheshire plain to the Welsh hills some 50 miles away. This is the England of half-timbered manor houses, feudal villages and high-yield dairy farms. It is a picture-book scene not readily associated with the North West in the eyes of strangers to the region.

What probably comes first to most is an altogether different image of the urban central area comprising Greater Manchester and Merseyside, Blackburn, Burnley and Preston. This is home to over five million people, as well as to most of the region's industry and commerce. Here, of course, is where the Industrial Revolution took off in the late eighteenth century, on the back of Lancashire's burgeoning cotton trade.

This is the most densely-populated part of Britain outside London. It has to cope with the dynamics of contemporary life while, at the same time, implementing long and medium-term plans to improve an environment which still bears scars from the revolution which began over two centuries ago.

Opposite A typical Lake District scene: Buttermere and Fleetwith Pike viewed from above Crummock Water.

25

Above The Castlerigg stone circle is a ring of 38 stones surrounded by the magnificent landscape of the Cumbrian mountains. The 5,000-year-old circle, near Keswick, is on National Trust land and is visited by thousands of people each year.

Examples of the former are the growth of Manchester Airport, an international hub central to the region's commercial vitality, built in classic urban fringe country between the mass housing of Wythenshawe and a delightful small-scale Cheshire valley. A good example of the latter is the Mersey Basin Campaign with its associated projects. Both are fundamental to the future of England's North West.

The Mersey Basin Campaign has been developing since 1985, having been devised as a means of combining the muscle of central and local government, industry, commerce and voluntary organisations to tackle the aftermath of land and water over-exploitation.

The campaign has been the catalyst for a range of initiatives now backed by the Northwest Development Agency, the North West Regional Assembly, Sustainability North West, English Partnerships, the Countryside Commission and English Nature. Before long it proved that real results could be achieved by the pooling of ideas and resources. It overcame the natural reluctance of Greater Manchester, Merseyside, Lancashire and Cheshire to work with each other. It staked out areas for co-operation which have led towards genuine regional policies and actions.

It's logical, really. The several headwaters of the River Mersey lie in Lancashire, North Derbyshire and Cheshire. Together they form what was one of Europe's most polluted rivers, as it meanders around South Manchester and across the Cheshire plain towards Liverpool Bay (linked, umbilically, to the Manchester Ship Canal). They were, by and large, responsible for the pollution – whether it came from the mill towns of the East Pennines, the chemical plants of North Derbyshire, or the dairy farms of Cheshire. They got away with murder – murder of natural life in the river – because, given the state of the Mersey, one could not really raise fingers in blame.

Yet, fingers were raised and industries – or local authorities – made to account for themselves. Massive projects, part-financed by United Utilities, the privatised utility, have since provided highly efficient sewage treatment plants which have transformed the condition of the tidal Mersey. And nature responds. Just as when the Thames was cleaned a quarter of a century ago, migrant fish including salmon are returning to the Mersey and coarse fish are thriving. The days when, it was claimed, you had half an hour to live if you swallowed a mouthful of Mersey water at Didsbury, are now thankfully a thing of the past!

Above Early morning view across Derwent Water towards Borrowdale.

27

Above Grasmere and Dunmail Raise viewed from Loughrigg Terrace.

Opposite The impact of settlers on the landscape is ever-present. The Roman fort of Mediobogdum (now known as Hardknott Castle) was built in the second century AD, or possibly earlier, and was garrisoned by a cohort from Dalmatia.

At one and the same time, and under the same philosophy, river-banks and nearby countryside or urban areas have been cleared and regenerated. The Civic Trust for the North West showed the way with its Bollin Valley Partnership in Stockport in 1972 – the Bollin being a Mersey tributary. It proved that realistic planning, using whatever grant aid it could muster and the enthusiasm and muscle of local volunteers, could achieve miracles. The country parks created by projects such as this have become part of the recreational life of local residents, who thus now enjoy an outstanding quality of life.

Over one hundred initiatives, often co-ordinated by the Groundwork Trust, the national body created to harness the voluntary sector, were underway by the turn of the century. Three complementary coastal and water quality schemes, allied with strategic plans for the Dee Estuary and Mersey Estuary, all work towards the same end.

The regeneration of brownfield sites for housing and industry and the constraint of the Green Belt, have both served to check urban spread, maximising land use and protecting the area's open spaces.

Such has been the success of the Mersey Basin Campaign and associated projects that the region is now putting into place a landscape strategy called Greening the North West. This strategy has not arrived from nowhere. It embraces statutory local authority unitary development plans which themselves embraced county council planning proposals. But there is a growing awareness that landscape does not stop at local authority boundaries. Professionals and politicians from around the region have set out to unite the patchwork.

Since 1996, Professor John Handley of Manchester University has co-ordinated a team assembled from relevant Manchester and Liverpool university departments, working for Sustainability North West and the Countryside Commission. Their brief has covered the region as a whole, but many of the proposals inevitably concern the Mersey Basin area.

Above Bassenthwaite Lake is the most northerly lake in Cumbria and also one of the largest. At Mirehouse, on the west shore, there is a small open-air theatre, built in 1974 for the reading of 'Morte d'Arthur' to the Tennyson Society, at the place where it is thought that Tennyson, who often stayed at Mirehouse, composed much of the poem.

Opposite Lowside Farm and Scalesfell, near Threlkeld. The hill farmer has helped shape the landscape, needing toughness and courage to make a living in such a beautiful yet harsh environment.

Right Ennerdale Water, with Pillar to the east.

Opposite Stockley Bridge at the foot of Styhead Pass in Upper Borrowdale.

Implementation of community forests is likely to make the biggest visual difference to urban and urban fringe landscape in the coming years. Red Rose Forest — which stretches from the Medlock Valley of East Manchester to the other side of Wigan — will effectively reforest the river valleys with broadleaf trees and create a sizeable green core around Wigan Flashes. Recreational routes proposed by the former Greater Manchester Countryside Unit as long ago as 1984 will improve as the forest trees take shape.

To the west, the Mersey Forest, covering 430 square miles of Merseyside and North Cheshire has already, in the decade it has been underway, provided a 45 per cent increase in woodland cover. It aims to achieve 12 per cent woodland cover over the designated area by 2025, putting the area above the UK average, even though much of it is urban.

33

Opposite Silverdale is a quiet coastal village set against the backdrop of the Cumbrian hills. The salt marshes and limestone cliffs provide a varied habitat for plants and wildlife.

Left The North West has a superb network of rivers, draining from the Pennines into the Irish Sea. The River Hodder is typical and, like the Ribble, Lune, Wyre, Kent and others, is ideal for walking and fishing.

Such projects tie in with the strategy's key recommendations to develop an integrated greenspace network which values naturally vegetated areas and protects wildlife corridors. The aim is also to conserve and revitalise city parklands and open spaces and to promote a strategic approach to attacking derelict and contaminated land.

Sustainability North West was formed as the environmental arm of The North West Partnership, the public-private partnership, which prior to the development of the Northwest Development Agency took on a region-wide remit to improve both the reality and the image of the region as a whole. Creating a better landscape and environment has continued to be central to the region's economic strategy.

After all, it was the uncontrolled and unsustainable energies of the Industrial Revolution which begot the region's particular character. For the North West to make the most of its extraordinary assets, people and sectors must willingly work towards the same end. Signs are that this is just what is happening today.

Right The Ribble Valley is dominated by the looming mass of Pendle Hill. Below its summit are attractive villages such as Downham (known to film buffs as the village where 'Whistle Down the Wind' was filmed).

Right below Parbold Hill, a point of reference in the softer landscape of south west Lancashire.

Opposite Walking above Nelson in east Lancashire. Take a short walk out of most North West towns and you will find yourself in stunning countryside.

Opposite The National Trust nature reserve at Formby offers one of England's largest sand dune systems as well as an internationally important site for wildlife, including one of Britain's last thriving colonies of red squirrel.

Left The Dee estuary, looking towards the coastline of North Wales.

Left below The cliff walk at Thurstaston, on the Wirral Way.

Above Woods at Alderley Edge. Extensive tree planting schemes in the Mersey and Red Rose community forests, are projected to increase woodland cover in Merseyside, North Cheshire and Greater Manchester, to 12 per cent of total land area by the year 2025, which is double the current figure. Over 2,000 hectares of new woodland has been created in the Mersey Forest since 1991, with planting ranging from conifers on the Sefton coast to mixed broadleaves elsewhere. The Red Rose Forest has a target of 25 million new trees over a 40-year period.

Above Legend has it that King Arthur and his knights are sleeping under the Edge with their horses, ready to spring into action should England be threatened. Without doubt, Alderley Edge has a sense of enchantment, with glorious views across the Cheshire plain from its wooded plateau.

41

Above The hamlet of Macclesfield Forest is set amongst the hills of the east Pennines, and is a popular walking area. St Stephen's Church is famous for its rush-bearing service held every August.

Above Climb out of Macclesfield and head eastwards towards Buxton (and Derbyshire) and in the shadow of Shutlingsloe, you come across the wild and beautiful Wildboarclough, much loved by generations of walkers exchanging the noise and bustle of the towns for the soothing calls of curlews and skylarks.

history reinvented as heritage

Philip Radcliffe

'The lot is fallen unto me in a fair ground: yea, I have a goodly heritage.' Psalm 16, v.7

Heritage is part of us. It is something we inherit – and something we pass on to those who come after. As befits a true-born son of Lancashire, I was brought up within a stone's throw of a cotton mill. That mill chimney and Blackpool Tower were the twin totems of my early life – one signifying work, the other day trips to the seaside. The Tower is still there but the mill has been converted into a different sort of heritage – smart apartments.

I have spent my working life, and much of my leisure time, exploring my region, naturally absorbing the heritage, from weekends with the Wordsworths at Grasmere, to tracking astronauts and objects in outer space at the radio telescope at Jodrell Bank. In a way, that is just the sort of contrast which reflects the richness of our heritage, from Romantic poetry to the romance of advanced science. This is just one example – and there are thousands more.

The North West used to be described as a place which has always given itself the airs of a continent, and why not? It is steeped in history, noted for invention – and reinvention. History is very much part of our modern cities and towns.

Take Manchester's Castlefield, which has had so many reincarnations over the centuries, reflecting the roller-coaster of industrial and economic change since its birth as a Roman fort. It is now reborn as Britain's first Urban Heritage Park, a dauntingly formal label for a lively area, sporting refreshed waterways and walkways, classy apartments in old warehouses, designer pubs and café-bars and modern workplaces, housing new technology and new media companies.

"Who would have thought a pub in a derelict part of town would work?" reflected Jim Ramsbottom, the first entrepreneur to venture in. He answered for himself: "You learn to trust your instincts, whatever people say."

We look at the former docks in Liverpool and Salford – and see national centres of the creative and dramatic arts like the Tate and the Lowry, across the waters of Salford Quays from which the stunning architectural creation of the Imperial War Museum North is rising. Fifty years ago, a survey of the region by Frank Singleton recorded that it was 'dominated by man-made features like the Liver building, rising above the Mersey docks to salute the voyager, or the aspiring chimneys of the cotton towns, or the neo-Venetian warehouses along the River Irwell'. Well, the Liver building and the warehouses are physically still there, but now there is so much else besides.

As recently as 1980 the Albert Dock, the largest group of Grade I listed buildings in the country, stood derelict – and the Merseyside Development Corporation made it the centrepiece of its docklands regeneration strategy. Today the Albert Dock is home to the Merseyside Maritime Museum and Granada Television studios as well as the Tate, and a myriad of shops and restaurants, while the former docks around have been transformed into hotels, business parks and apartments.

Opposite Little Moreton Hall in Cheshire is astonishing, a perfect timber-framed building set haphazardly above a moat. Now owned by the National Trust, the fifteenth century hall is one of the notable attractions of the North West.

Water of the navigable kind has always had great importance to the North West, from the cities to the seaside to the Lakes. As early as 1660, there were suggestions that the Irwell and the Mersey should be made navigable, from the estuary to the city. Much later, men of vision saw the need for man-made canals, the grandest of them all being 'The Last Great Ditch' – the 35-mile stretch of the Manchester Ship Canal. The nation took notice and Queen Victoria herself came to open it in 1894. "It is to Lancashire, as the Nile is to Egypt," declared Alfred Watkin, a later chairman of the Manchester Ship Canal Company.

As well as the rivers and canals and seascape, we have the Lakes, with all their natural and cultural heritage. Special days in the Lakes stir the memory – family outings, sailing on Windermere, walking over Striding Edge, climbing Helvellyn, looking down on the wonder of Tarn Hows. Literary retreats, taking in that outstanding Wordsworth Museum adjacent to Dove Cottage at Grasmere, attract book lovers and collectors from all over the world. Yet part and parcel of those gatherings are the walks around the lake before breakfast, led by the poet's descendant, Jonathan, an Oxford academic. Thus are the natural and the cultural integrated, as they are also at Beatrix Potter's cottage near Hawkshead and at Brantwood, John Ruskin's house-museum.

Above According to legend, Pendragon Castle, in Cumbria, is where Uther Pendragon, father of King Arthur, died. In fact, the castle was built around 1173 and survived precariously until burnt by the Scots in 1341. Rebuilt and burned down again (this time accidentally), the castle ruins are sited dramatically in the Mallerstang Valley in the shadow of the forbidding Wild Boar Fell.

Opposite Beeston Castle is a reminder of the frequent battles and skirmishes which marked the history of this vulnerable border area. After falling to Parliamentary forces in 1643, the castle fell into disuse and remains a picturesque ruin standing high above the Cheshire plain.

47

Above Designed by Samuel Wyatt in 1791, Tatton Hall, former seat of the Egerton family, is set in 2,000 acres of parkland. Now owned by The National Trust and managed by Cheshire County Council, the Hall and Park, on the fringe of Knutsford, are open to the public, who can only marvel that such a magnificent estate was the preserve of just one family. A perfect film set, the Hall has regularly been used as a setting for period dramas.

It is odd to think now that Cumbria and much of north Lancashire were once part of the kingdom of Strathclyde and then of Northumbria. Only after 1092, when Carlisle was wrested from the Scots by William Rufus, was it ready to be part of England. Henry I, his brother, visited Carlisle in 1122 – and established a bishopric there, bringing the North West into the Norman system and leading to the foundation of monasteries and the building of fine churches.

Behind the fine old church at Kirkby Lonsdale is that river view which John Ruskin described as the most beautiful in the world. Ruskin's View, my personal favourite, looks down on the sweep of the magnificent River Lune, which rises in the high Pennines, flows towards you, way down below, and then rushes into the distance.

By the time the Lune reaches the sea, it brings us to the county town, Lancaster – and to yet more history. The castle, dating back to a stronghold built by the Normans against the Scots, was rebuilt in the eighteenth and nineteenth centuries. From the Lady Ashton memorial, on the city's outskirts, it is said that 'seven counties, mountains, plain and sea can be surveyed'.

Above The Drawing Room, Bramall Hall. Another of the region's magnificent country houses, Bramall Hall retains its Tudor character although it was substantially remodelled in the nineteenth century. Recently discovered under later paintwork, its sixteenth century wall paintings are regarded as some of the most important in the country. Set in landscaped gardens, the Hall dominates the valley of Micker Brook, near Stockport.

Right Weavers' Triangle, in Burnley, is an impressive scheme aimed at preserving an essential part of the town's history. The Triangle lies along a section of the Leeds and Liverpool Canal which was used to transport raw cotton and finished goods. The textile mills and factories that line the canal present a complete picture of the time when Burnley led the world in weaving cotton cloth and The Weavers' Triangle Trust is gradually restoring the area, which includes weaving sheds, spinning mills, warehouses, domestic buildings and a school.

Opposite The North West has a unique railway heritage. The Manchester to Liverpool railway was the first passenger line in the world (Edge Hill station in Liverpool is the world's oldest passenger railway station). The East Lancashire Railway is an enthusiast's dream, operated by volunteers, with eight miles of operational track between Bury and Rawtenstall.

As with Lancaster, there is much to admire in that other ancient county town, Chester, and its beautiful river, the Dee. The mediaeval architecture, the Rows and the walkway on the wall, are justly famed. Tourists – many Americans to my certain knowledge – flock there. And we who have known it from childhood, not least because of the zoo, never tire of it. One of the greatest pleasures, during the annual Summer Music Festival, is to hear soaring choral music in the Anglican Cathedral, that magnificent church which has been echoing to such sounds for almost a thousand years.

51

In this part of the region, you are in a different part of the 'continent', the Cheshire plain. Draw a diagonal across it, say from Lancaster to Macclesfield, and you can see and feel the difference. To the east is an agricultural plain, to the west the hills. In a way, it is the difference between silk and cotton.

Standing on top of the Cloud, that aptly-named, 1,000ft hill near Congleton, you get a wonderful view of the plain, from the Potteries to the Pennines. Nearby is the place famed for silk manufacture, Macclesfield, with its Heritage Centre, telling the history of silk and, incidentally, providing a cosy venue for the excellent Northern Chamber Orchestra.

Not that cotton is forgotten. The preserved model village of Quarry Bank at Styal, near Manchester Airport, founded in 1784, is now an award-winning working museum run by the National Trust, with spinning room, weaving shed and giant water wheel.

Above Cheshire's villages are famous for their picture postcard charm. Great Budworth is no exception, with its magnificent Church of St Mary and All Saints and fine period buildings.

Opposite The North West's heritage runs deep; from castles to cities, churches to canals. The townscape can be savoured, as can the rural, including secluded hamlets such as Wincle near Macclesfield.

53

Above Lewis Carroll was well acquainted with St Wilfrid's Church in Grappenhall, near Warrington, which is noted for its carving of a cat above the west window. Thought to be the proverbial Cheshire Cat, the curious feline makes its appearance in 'Alice's Adventures in Wonderland'.

Opposite Prestbury is a small village at the foot of the Pennines. It has repeatedly won 'Best Kept Village' awards and boasts a beautiful thirteenth century church.

Think of Cheshire, though, and you immediately envisage picturesque, black-and-white, half-timbered houses. We all have our favourites, like Little Moreton Hall, built in the fifteenth century; the Elizabethan Bramall Hall, with its remarkable wall paintings of beasts and demons in the ballroom; and Gawsworth Hall, a crowd-pulling venue for open-air opera and drama.

The culture stakes are high in this rural part of the region. Not far from Gawsworth – and, in contrast, practically in the shadow of Jodrell Bank – is Clonter Opera Farm, now established as the Glyndebourne of the North and noted not only for its productions, but also for its nurturing of talented young singers.

Interestingly, film-makers, particularly of classical adaptations, have been quick to put grand family houses hereabouts on the map again. Lyme Hall, with its deer-populated parkland,

featured in *Pride and Prejudice* on BBC Television. It was in Lyme's lake that Darcy (Colin Firth) soaked his shirt – and set the nation's female population all a-flutter. Together with Knutsford's Arley Hall, Lyme was also a backcloth for the 2002 Granada Television adaptation of *The Forsyte Saga*. Nearby, Tatton Park's eighteenth century mansion featured in Granada's award-winning *Brideshead Revisited*. So, the old estates add another claim to fame through contemporary media.

One of the joys of the region is the constant link between old and new, between industry and culture. This is arguably nowhere better exemplified than in the invention, enterprise and philanthropy of a man from Bolton, William Hesketh Lever, born in 1851. He built an industrial empire out of soap – and became the first Lord Leverhulme.

He is the link between Bolton and Port Sunlight; Bolton School and the Lady Lever Art Gallery, with its outstanding collection of eighteenth century paintings and furniture; the wild, natural beauty of Rivington and the well-planned 130-acre garden village for his workers on the Wirral Peninsula; the Tudor house, Hall-i'-th'-Wood, home of Samuel Crompton, inventor of the spinning mule; and the Queen Anne-style Bluecoat Chambers in Liverpool, which he saved for the city. Those are only part of his legacy. That's heritage.

Above Parkgate is a port without the sea. Unfortunately, the Dee estuary gradually silted up, leaving this once important embarkation point for Ireland high and dry. Famous people stayed here including Nelson's Lady Hamilton, as well as Handel, prior to the first performance of his 'Messiah' in Dublin. Occasionally, at high tide, the River Dee still laps against the promenade walls.

Opposite Liverpool's Bluecoat Chambers is the oldest building in the city centre. Built between 1717 and 1725, it was saved for the nation through the generosity of William Lever, the first Lord Leverhulme, who wished to turn the building into a great centre for the arts. The Bluecoat, for a time the home of Liverpool University's School of Architecture, now houses an art gallery, concert hall and other art related businesses.

57

Opposite The doorway of St Bees Priory in Cumbria was named after St Bega, an Irish princess who landed here in about 900 AD to avoid enforced marriage to a Viking chieftain. The twelfth century church with its superb Norman doorway is one of many magnificent examples of early Christian architecture which survive in the North West.

Left The beautiful thirteenth century doorway to the Norman chapel, part of St Peter's Church in Prestbury, near Macclesfield.

59

Right The Ruskin Rooms, Knutsford. Elizabeth Gaskell's home town was named after Canute, King of England 994-1035, who supposedly forded the stream here, thus giving the town its name – Cunetsford (as it appeared in the Domesday Book). Built by individualistic architect Richard Harding Watt, in 1902, the Ruskin Rooms were used by General George Patton in 1944, when the US Third Army was stationed at nearby Peover Hall.

Right below Wycoller Hall, near Colne, a picturesque ruin, the inspiration for Ferndean Manor in 'Jane Eyre'.

Opposite Grasmere, home to William Wordsworth from 1799 to 1808.

The North West boasts many important literary connections. William Wordsworth is synonymous with the Lake District, particularly Grasmere and Dove Cottage. An intriguing connection has the Jesuit college at Stoneyhurst and the Ribble Valley as the inspiration and geography for JRR Tolkien's 'Lord of the Rings'. Less speculative is the evidence that Shakespeare spent time at Hoghton, moving around the great Catholic families of Lancashire, or the influence of Daresbury, in Cheshire, on a young Charles Dodgson, better known as Lewis Carroll, author of 'Alice in Wonderland'.

Whilst the lakes and fells provided inspiration for Wordsworth and Beatrix Potter, the hard life faced by the poor in nineteenth century Manchester and its surrounding towns inspired Knutsford's Elizabeth Gaskell to write 'Cranford', 'North and South' and other ground-breaking novels. Her acclaimed biography of her friends, the Brontë sisters, was also a critical success.

61

Opposite Quarry Bank Mill is in the shadow of Manchester International Airport. Now owned by the National Trust, the former cotton mill and nearby Styal village were the inspiration of Samuel Greg, a humanitarian industrialist who took in boys and girls from orphanages and workhouses and housed and fed them in a purpose-built Apprentices' House. The mill closed in 1959 but has been reopened as a working museum, with weaving and other skills on daily display.

Left Wigan Pier was a pioneer example of how to turn a redundant industrial site into a major tourist attraction. A derelict industrial wharf on the Leeds and Liverpool Canal was transformed into a heritage attraction which includes a resident theatre company, cotton spinning, the world's largest working mill steam engine and the Opie Museum of Memories, a fascinating collection of twentieth century packaging and ephemera.

Left below Bollington, near Macclesfield, is a typical mill town, one of many small urban centres found throughout the North West. Such communities grew rapidly during the Industrial Revolution and the legacy of the eighteenth and nineteenth centuries is an important and often attractive part of the North West landscape.

a townscape renewed

Peter Elson

'God made the country, and man made the town.' William Cowper

England's architecture is encapsulated in the North West's rich townscapes. Every style, from fortress to factory via the villa and village vernacular, is to be found in this immensely diverse region. Its foundations spring from the highly varied topography: the Cheshire plain, the Pennine foothills, the Lake District, the Lancashire and Cumbria coastlines. From within comes the region's natural leitmotif, the rich sandstone running through its centre, uniting the great border cities of Chester in the south and Carlisle in the north. It is a building material as evocative of the area as magpie half-timbering. Around the North West the street plans of many towns were dictated by their Roman or mediaeval origins.

Other natural resources helped create the Industrial Revolution with its urgent need for factories, mills and cheap homes for workers on a hitherto unknown scale. This surge of wealth also led to swathes of more glamorous buildings and symbols of new pride like Blackburn Cotton Exchange and Blackpool Tower.

Neither should we forget the influence on building styles of the dominant landowning families such as the Grosvenors (Dukes of Westminster) in Cheshire, the Stanleys (Earls of Derby) in Lancashire and the Lowthers (Earls of Lonsdale) in Cumbria.

However, there has been the equally powerful, but more abstract, unifying emotional drive often overlooked in the North West's development. The sheer range of the region's building stock has masked this vital theme: the desire for improvement. The belief in 'getting on' is an old one, deeply ingrained in the North West's psyche to the extent that it was successfully satirised before the First World War in Harold Brighouse's Salford-set comedy, *Hobson's Choice.*

Such aspirational behaviour not only applied to individuals. Much earlier, as the British Empire burgeoned, towns like Lancaster and Whitehaven in the eighteenth century were well-placed to trade with the new markets of the Americas and the Caribbean. Whitehaven, developed by the Lowthers as a coal port, was laid out in American gridiron-pattern, making it one of northern Britain's first planned towns. An astonishing 250 Georgian and Victorian buildings are listed there by English Heritage.

Plain functionality was not enough. Industrial buildings and engineering constructions had to create a lasting impression. The leading canal engineer John Rennie's Whitehaven Harbour Pier stands testament to the port's status as the world's leading centre of shipbuilding in the early nineteenth century – long after steamships took trade to the deeper Mersey waters. While Lancaster is dominated by the elevated thirteenth century castle on the site of a Roman fort and the eleventh century Priory Church of St Mary, transatlantic commerce imported materials like Cuban mahogany, which spawned a cabinet-making industry and a new highly-skilled working class.

Opposite Blackpool is the most visited seaside resort in Britain. A brash and colourful town, it has always fought to stay at the top of its trade. The 518 foot Tower, erected in 1894, was an instant success with the mill and factory workers who flocked to the resort for a well earned respite from their hard lives. Amusement arcades, theatres and even a zoo ensured a good time was guaranteed and this philosophy to please has constantly pushed Blackpool into reinventing itself.

Above Maryport is a quiet town on the Cumbrian coast, once a busy trading port. The harbour is now given over to a small fishing fleet and strenuous efforts are being made to attract tourism, which has largely overlooked this attractive town.

Unlike contemporary developers, yesterday's speculators and architects needed a classical appreciation of the arts. Lancaster's new wealth permitted northern replicas of the fashionable new Georgian squares in London and Bath.

With industry and money came mass transport and leisure. Responding to demand, seaside resorts were developed, both popular and up-market. Once, nowhere was more refined than Southport. With a reputation stoked by rich Liverpool merchants and Lancashire's cottonocracy, by 1855 some 40,000 visitors were arriving daily by train.

Lord Street, its central boulevard, remains a by-word for gracious living, with glamorous shops, glass awnings, vaulted arcades and former hydro hotels. The architectural historian, Professor Quentin Hughes, believes it is not outrageous to compare it with the Champs Elysées. His research reveals that Baron Haussman's rebuilding of Paris was probably inspired by discussions with the former Lord Street resident, Emperor Napoleon III.

Blackpool had no time for such 'lah-di-dah' attitudes. Yet the instantly recognisable symbol of the resort is also linked with Paris, that superb flourish of civic confidence, the Tower. Built in 1894, this Eiffel-inspired offspring bestrides a ballroom, aquarium and indoor circus, helping to turn barren Lancashire sand dunes into the country's most popular resort.

Like the Tower, Blackpool's Winter Gardens blend sumptuous seaside Victoriana with, surprisingly, pre-war Art Deco. Both complexes were partly designed by Britain's greatest theatre designer, Frank Matcham, whose other work here is the exquisite Grand Theatre. Three nineteenth century piers and the 40-acre Pleasure Beach (with its latest sensation, the Pepsi Max roller-coaster) are joined by the curving esplanade. Plied by bucking emerald and cream-painted period trams, the resort is also known for its autumn illuminations.

In the nineteenth century, old styles were plundered with gusto and 'improved' for industrial, civic and domestic architecture. The Victorians combined romantic appearance and mass

Above and opposite Preston's coat of arms bears the initials PP. Whatever their historic meaning, they now stand for Proud Preston, a fitting epitaph to a fine town with a reputation for thrusting enterprise. The seeds of success are evident: a bustling marina, the magnificent Harris Museum and Art Gallery and its own seat of higher education, the University of Central Lancashire. Preston was elevated to city status in 2002 as part of the Queen's Golden Jubilee celebrations.

production. Again, these progressive methods were harnessed for the purpose of self-aggrandisement.

Chester, the prosperous county town of Cheshire, presents a mediaeval appearance surrounded by walls largely built on Roman foundations. Yet much of this picturesque work is Victorian, including the cathedral's exterior, remodelled by George Gilbert Scott between 1868 and 1876.

Paradoxically, Chester's older properties look newer, having been re-faced over the centuries. What appears Georgian is mediaeval and what looks like Tudor half-timbering is Victorian, immediately detectable by its larger proportions. It may be fake, but the quality of architecture (by the likes of John Douglas) and construction (bank-rolled by the Grosvenors) is outstanding.

69

This make-over extends to the city's most unusual feature, the Rows. These are first-floor open-galleried shopfronts stretching along the four original Roman cruciform-plan streets of Eastgate, Northgate, Watergate and Bridge Street. This attractive curiosity was developed around the thirteenth century, either as a defensive measure against the marauding Welsh, or on the solid Roman ruins bordering the roadsides.

Original Tudor buildings are best seen in Nantwich, dating from the town's rebuilding after a fire in 1583 which was so damaging that Queen Elizabeth I spearheaded the rescue fund. A gentrified former Cheshire salt town and stagecoach stop, it was eclipsed by the purpose-built railway town of Crewe. St Mary's fine fourteenth century church, with its octagonal tower, was happily spared from the fire, as was Churche's Mansion, of 1577, and Sweetbriar Hall, of 1450.

In contrast, Macclesfield, set on a bluff at the edge of the Pennines, was once the centre of the English silk industry. Amid the swirl of modern traffic, it retains a small, Georgian market town intimacy. This is a time-capsule of an early industrial era with old mills, terraced cottages and nonconformist churches, set on a mediaeval street layout.

Above Bolton is true Lancashire, deeply rooted in tradition yet progressively minded when it comes to change. The civic pride is evident in the grand Town Hall and surrounding buildings. Here was the home of those great innovators, Richard Arkwright and Samuel Crompton, who helped revolutionise the cotton industry. The textile industry may have declined but Bolton has looked to the future, epitomised by the new Reebok stadium, home to Bolton Wanderers, founder members of the Football League.

Opposite The striking, cast-iron canopy of Bolton Market.

Above It has been claimed by Professor Quentin Hughes that Napoleon III was so impressed by his trip to Southport that he decided to redesign Paris on the same principle of wide boulevards. Fanciful, perhaps, but the town has an air of up-market elegance that few other seaside resorts can match.

Warrington was hammered into its present form by heavy industry. Attractive corners survive, and its Town Hall is exquisite. Designed by James Gibbs as a mansion in 1750, it was later acquired by the town council. The Sankey Street gilded cast iron gates were displayed at the Great Exhibition of 1851, and were originally intended as a gift for Queen Victoria.

Beneath the brooding mass of Pendle Hill, Blackburn was formerly the world's greatest cotton weaving centre. That the town's population rose tenfold between 1801 and 1900 (from 11,980 to 108,865) shows the seismic change in Lancashire wrought by the Industrial Revolution. The switch from hand-weaving to steam power-looms, concentrating workers in the lower valleys, has left the town a legacy of weaving sheds, mill buildings and chimneys.

Cramming thousands of workers into homes near the mills gave rise to the North West's familiar miles of terraced houses. Where there is muck and brass in Lancashire there is also a grand town hall. Civic pride in Blackburn demanded an 1850 design resembling London's Old Mansion House. Later, the town's Gothic parish church was enlarged into a cathedral dating from 1926.

Preston's name derives from Priests' Town and it has been for centuries home to Britain's largest indigenous Roman Catholic population, with the tall spire of St Walburge's pointing the way heavenwards. Victorian town planning values are represented by the functionality of the old market, the pomp of the town hall, the green lung of Avenham Park and the neoclassicism of the Harris Museum & Art Gallery.

Carlisle's leisurely pace belies a chequered and often bloody history. The cathedral, castle and fragments of the city walls survive, but the city's ambience owes more to its nineteenth century industrial growth and modern administrative functions. The lopsided, red sandstone cathedral, dating from the eleventh century, may be England's smallest, but it looms over the city.

Carlisle Castle, guardian of the Anglo-Scottish border, contains one of England's finest Norman keeps. The defensive style continued with the two huge drum-towers of Telford and Smirke's 1807 county buildings and court house. The Victorian age gave us the magnificent Citadel railway station (junction for seven railway companies' lines) and the bustling covered market. Other Cumbrian market towns like Penrith are essentially miniature versions of Carlisle.

Above Warrington is one of the fastest growing towns in Britain. Equidistant between Liverpool and Manchester and at the hub of the motorway network, it is ideally placed to benefit from a host of distributive and other service businesses. Impressive business parks and retail outlets have driven the town's expansion to a degree where its history is perhaps overlooked. But what other town can boast so fine a Town Hall with such magnificent gates?

73

Above The Anglo-Saxon term for salt-works is 'wich' and Nantwich, along with Northwich and Middlewich, grew rich on its extraction. The wealth it generated is reflected in its mediaeval buildings, particularly St Mary's Church (the 'Cathedral of South Cheshire'). Today, Nantwich has a more varied economy with a strong agricultural industry, retailing, tourism and other service industries.

What of the future? Traditional industries have receded faster than the tide at Southport, but redundant old buildings are finding new uses. Southport itself has successfully converted its redbrick Gothic seafront hospital into a glamorous apartment complex, an idea unthinkable a decade ago. Warehouses and mills alongside the Leeds and Liverpool Canal at Eanam Wharf in Blackburn and the Shropshire Union Canal in Chester have been refurbished as upmarket offices and a hotel. Whitehaven's conservation area includes the Beacon, with its Meteorological Office Weather Gallery, along with other interesting features.

Above The elegant suspension bridge, opened in 1961, links Widnes to Runcorn, now largely a new town and a major centre of the chemical industry.

Above With centuries of history on show, Chester is the most complete walled city in Britain. The mediaeval Rows, substantially rebuilt by the Victorians, give the heart of Chester a unique appeal. Add St Werburgh's Cathedral, nearby Chester Zoo, magnificent shops and boating on the River Dee, and one can understand why the city retains its position as a top international attraction.

Opposite A salmon boat on the banks of the River Dee near Chester's Old Bridge.

The North West's enthusiasm for imaginative construction continues unabated with projects like Lancaster's Millennium Bridge. The old municipal dreams of enhanced status still drive our leading towns as they plan their future in a new century. Preston was raised to city status in 2002 as part of the Queen's Golden Jubilee celebrations, with six other local authorities – Blackburn with Darwen, Blackpool, Bolton, Stockport, Warrington and Wirral – having similar aspirations. Promotion to a city, it is hoped, will increase Preston's national and international profile and boost the marketing potential of the surrounding area.

Preston has already revamped its docks as a successful marina. Also impressive are the National Football Museum and the transformation of Preston Polytechnic into the University of Central Lancashire, now the UK's seventh largest university.

78 *Above The attractive market town of Sandbach is renowned for its ancient crosses which stand in the cobbled Market Square. The weekly market, held every Thursday, has existed since the days of Elizabeth I and attracts visitors from miles around.*

Since the 1960s Chester has striven to be the North West's premier shopping centre, based on the city's Grosvenor Precinct. This has now been upgraded to compete with purpose-built US-style malls like Manchester's Trafford Centre.

Another imported American idea may entirely change the face of our biggest resort, if Blackpool's flirtation with the proposal to become Britain's biggest gambling resort turns into a full-blown Las Vegas affair. There's no end to self-improvement.

Above Close to the motorway network and Manchester International Airport and set in glorious countryside, Knutsford is one of the most prosperous towns in Britain, with low unemployment and a thriving economy.

79

Right and opposite Lancaster is the old county town of Lancashire and has a history commensurate with its position. Its Norman castle was built upon an earlier Roman fortification and the town is crammed with reminders of its illustrious past. Dominating the skyline is the Ashton Memorial, erected by James Ashton, a linoleum millionaire, to his wife. Lancaster is a thriving town, with an excellent university and superb countryside on its doorstep.

Right below Whitehaven is a Georgian gem of a town. In the early eighteenth century, it was second only to London in export tonnage. Its connection with America began in 1683, trading coal for tobacco, a lucrative arrangement which ensured Whitehaven's growth. Settlers from the town left for the new colony, amongst them the Washington family. Mildred Washington, grandmother of George Washington, is buried in the grounds of St Nicholas' Church. The port was also the only place in Britain to be attacked by American naval forces when, in 1778, during the American War of Independence, John Paul Jones unsuccessfully attempted to set the merchant fleet on fire. Today, the harbour area has been regenerated and the Georgian heritage is being restored.

manchester and liverpool
cities of tomorrow

Sir Bob Scott

'Have nothing in your houses that you do not know to be useful, or believe to be beautiful.' William Morris

For over twenty years I worked in Manchester and observed Liverpool. Then for five years I worked in London and observed Manchester and Liverpool. For the past three years I have been working in Liverpool and observing Manchester. I feel I know the North West from the inside pretty well and, importantly, I have studied the North West from the perspective of London. My conclusion is that Liverpool thinks about itself, Manchester thinks about London, and London does not give Liverpool or Manchester a thought. Football is different. I'll come to that later.

The relationship between Liverpool, Manchester and London is an issue which cannot be avoided. Britain is not like Germany, Spain, Italy, the US, Canada or Australia, each with several first class cities of which one, often the least distinguished, is the capital. France is the nearest equivalent, but even Paris is overshadowed by London. The UK has a world-class capital and several major cities, of which Manchester and Liverpool are two. However – apart from Edinburgh and Cardiff – they are not recognised as regional capitals. So they have been unable to compete, not only with London, but with supposedly comparable regional capitals like Barcelona, Munich, Sydney and Toronto. It is not a matter of size so much as government.

How do our two cities match up today? Do they have the basic ingredients in sufficient quantity to make up a successful twin-city region? What unique qualities does each have that can give flesh to the hope that the region can be a recognisable player one day like Catalonia or Bavaria or New South Wales? To those who scoff at such an ambition I would merely point out that the South's confidence in entering the American Civil War against the North was based on a conviction that the might of the Lancashire cotton magnates would enter the war on their side. Nobody doubts the ancient muscle of these two powerhouse cities of the nineteenth century. But it is how they measure up for the twenty-first that matters now.

Manchester first. By Manchester I mean Greater Manchester, not the smallish city itself, and by Liverpool I mean Merseyside. I am sorry if that offends Salford, Rochdale, St Helens, Birkenhead and the others, but when a man from Trafford is abroad he says he comes from Manchester and that is the line I take here. It is clear that Manchester is stronger than Liverpool. It has almost twice the population. It is an inland conurbation with a rounded hinterland and two-hour access for a third of the entire country. It has a world-class international airport. Its transport system is gradually improving, probably a little faster than elsewhere in a country which has fallen badly behind its competitors in this respect. Metrolink, the on-street tram system, is widely admired, but road and rail infrastructure still needs massive improvement, especially in its links with London and the South East and into mainland Europe.

Opposite Liverpool's waterfront is one of the most distinctive in the world. The 'Three Graces' (The Royal Liver Building, Cunard Building and Port of Liverpool Building) are a magnificent sight, particularly when viewed from the deck of one of the famous Mersey ferries.

Above Manchester's Metrolink, the on-street tram system, has been a great success and is the envy of many other cities.

Opposite The Victoria, Salford Quays, an imaginative Peel Holdings development, makes the most of its dramatic waterside setting and has been instrumental in encouraging similar high profile developments.

There has been significant investment in Manchester as a conference city, along with a recent surge in hotel development. By night, streets are becoming busier and busier, with a welcome emphasis on city centre living. Recovery from the 1996 IRA bomb, which devastated much of the commercial city centre, could not have been more remarkable. Manchester has a sizeable business and professional community without coming out of the London shadow. It has four excellent universities, a respected business school, a seriously good music college and several exceptional high schools. Manchester is considered to be a great city in which to be young, yet many of its most talented offspring still move south to find fame and fortune.

Cultural life is constantly improving. At its best it is magnificent, but opera and dance are thin on the ground and wholly imported. Granada Television remains a world-leader but, like almost every native-born industry, Granada has moved its headquarters to London. National newspapers which once published proud northern editions from Manchester, now only print there, if that. All the same, the past decade has seen a remarkable investment in culture. A city which boasts the Bridgewater Hall, the Hallé Orchestra, the BBC Philharmonic, the Lowry, the Imperial War

Museum North, a rebuilt and extended City Art Gallery, the Whitworth Art Gallery, the Science and Industry Museum, the Royal Exchange Theatre, the Cornerhouse, the Palace Theatre and the Opera House, as well as the new Urbis Centre, can be considered rich indeed. No city has created more benefit from the millions showered down by the various arms of the National Lottery.

Meanwhile sport is enjoying a golden age. Manchester United is a phenomenal world force, while the staging of the 2002 Commonwealth Games has brought international focus and a clutch of brand-new sports buildings to the city for future generations. The new stadium and swimming complex along with the MEN Arena, the Velodrome, G-Mex and the two Old Traffords (the second, the home of Lancashire County Cricket Club, stages Test matches) all mean that Manchester stands comparison with any sports capital in the world. Indeed, sport is the most coherent symbol of the region, and in fervour if not in facilities, Liverpool is Manchester's equal.

England is a federal country in one way only – football. When it comes to football, London is simply another British city. Liverpool and Anfield give not an inch to United and Old Trafford and no other club dares to try that line. When you add Everton, Manchester City, Bolton, Blackburn,

Above Sleek and modern, Urbis is the focal point of the Millennium Quarter, a £41m project incorporating land bordered by the River Irwell. Six floors will contain exhibitions on the city's history and future.

Opposite The triple-tiered dome of the new Triangle shopping complex literally floods the building with light. The effect is enhanced by the extensive use of glass: in the cylindrical lift, the spiral staircase and the transparent escalators. Built from the shell of the Corn and Produce Exchange, bombed by the IRA in 1996, the Triangle is a potent symbol of Manchester's regeneration. Filled with exclusive shops selling designer clothes and fashionable furniture, this is no ordinary mall, but another important piece in the Manchester shopping jigsaw.

87

Right The design and construction of monumental St George's Hall, in the centre of Liverpool, represent the lifetime's work of its young architect, Harvey Lonsdale Elmes. The massive structure so preoccupied him that it sapped all his energies and he died of consumption at the age of only 33.

Opposite Whether illuminated at night, bathed in sunlight, or shrouded in mist from the River Mersey, the two Liverpool cathedrals tower majestically over the city at either end of Hope Street. The modern lines of the Metropolitan Cathedral contrast strikingly with its mammoth sandstone counterpart.

Burnley, Preston and the rest, you are talking about the game's most passionate following. Both codes of rugby flourish. Sale has emerged as a top professional Rugby Union club; St Helens and Wigan are Rugby League's most evocative names. Rivalry between top sports clubs is sometimes offered as a reason why the North West region will never come together. This is nonsense. Local derbies, indeed any robust type of sub-regional competition, serve to strengthen the body regional. It makes it tougher and gives the region an added dimension.

While Manchester's revival over the past 20 years has been steady, solid and occasionally spectacular, Liverpool's has only just started. The hole from which it is emerging was partly self-dug, much deeper, and the problems more profound than Manchester's. Major port cities around the world have well-known regeneration problems and Liverpool's difficulties have been as intense as anywhere.

What is fascinating to a relative newcomer to Liverpool like myself – who had been, it is true, a sympathetic spectator just 30 miles down the East Lancs Road during the 1970s and 1980s – is that in crucial ways the raw material for renaissance is more potent in Liverpool than in

89

Manchester. I would never have been persuaded of this without coming to work in the city and putting some roots down. Liverpool makes little attempt to sell itself to outsiders; you have to find out for yourself.

The Liverpool audit is confusing compared with Manchester. For a start, Liverpool is beautiful and exceedingly elegant. The majesty of the place is never far from a scruffy corner. All the same, scruffiness is relatively easy to deal with. Creating grandeur is harder.

Liverpool, with truly majestic assets, has, until recently, grossly undervalued them. Museums, galleries and music are magnificently served. The Walker is not simply a splendid city art gallery, it is the National Gallery of the North of England. The Liverpool Museum has recently undergone a transformation with the largest single Heritage Lottery grant ever made. No English city has the equivalent of the William Brown Street group of Classical Victorian buildings. The Royal Liverpool Philharmonic Hall and Orchestra, the Merseyside Maritime Museum, the Lady Lever Gallery and the Conservation Centre are all leaders. With the Beatles, Liverpool has a unique position in twentieth

Above This view, with the traditional Glasgow Assurance Building in the foreground and the stylish Observatory behind, typifies the old and new within the city of Manchester.

Opposite This Grade II listed building in Portland Street, Manchester, was saved from demolition as a result of a campaign by Lady Eleanor Campbell-Orde, the senior surviving member of the Watts family. The warehouse was then bought by the Britannia Hotels group in 1979, who converted it into a 338 bed hotel, which opened its doors in 1982. An exceptional feature of the building is that the windows on each floor are of a different architectural style.

century popular culture. The Beatles are the city's most famous icons but we are only now beginning adequately to celebrate them. At last there are plans for proper recognition taking shape.

The city council leadership and Liverpool Vision now have a new sense of purpose and are transmitting a new air of confidence. But much remains to be done. The streetscape is magnificent but too many buildings are empty. There are pockets of pulsating night-life but much of the city at night is provincially quiet. The waterfront has been included in a select list of new World Heritage Sites, but acres of it await development.

The process of people choosing to live in city centres, in new housing and flats in converted warehouses, is happening everywhere – especially Manchester – but Liverpool is the last of the major cities to experience it. Liverpool must be the only major city in Europe whose infrastructure has been constructed for a population twice its present size. The road lay-out is generous and the underground rail system extensive. In modern terms, the city has tremendous spare capacity.

Above Manchester's waterways, so long neglected, have now, at last, been recognised as an important urban resource. Scenes such as this, more reminiscent of Amsterdam than of inner city Manchester, are now commonplace in the city.

Opposite Manchester's canals and waterways have been systematically cleaned up and brought back to life, providing lively areas such as Castlefield, in which to shop, eat, drink and relax.

The city's professional community is smaller than in its heyday, but the sense of revival is tangible. Land values, house prices and office rents are rising at a rate above the national average. Liverpool's bid to be European Capital of Culture, after a quiet start, has been adopted by leading players from all sectors as a standard bearer of the city's new view of itself.

Liverpool is a city which tends to look back to its glory days. It is true that you cannot understand the present and construct the future without knowing the past. Like Venice, or Prague, or Naples, Liverpool's history is almost overpowering and can be an inhibition against modern planning. Liverpool has more statutorily protected buildings than any city outside London and local pride in its public realm is intense. One could argue that the finest individual buildings in Britain of the nineteenth and twentieth centuries are both in Liverpool – St George's Hall (completed in 1854) and the Anglican Cathedral (finally consecrated in 1986).

These buildings do not simply represent great architecture. They reveal a crucial theme that always has and still does run through Liverpool's psyche: a creativity which is youthful,

95

unstoppable, humorous and aggressive. For what is less well known is that both buildings were put out to national competition and won by incredibly young architects. Harvey Elmes, the architect of St George's Hall, was just 23 when he won the competition and Gilbert Scott, the architect of the cathedral, a mere 25.

It is part of Liverpool's fearlessness and encouragement of talent and creativity that such young men should have won these prestigious open competitions. The forceful young are still a constant factor in Liverpool life. Elmes or Scott, Paul McCartney or Michael Owen, Cilla Black or Willy Russell, Simon Rattle or Beryl Bainbridge, they start young and they succeed young in Liverpool's fertile soil. The pity is they so often move away. Nevertheless, this self-seeding, raw talent is a major contribution to the mix for a potent region. It is alive and flourishing. The new industries are Liverpool's new strength. In independent television and film-making, in the invention of computer games, in companies like Wade-Smith, Amaze and Urban Splash, in web design companies, in new music-making, in Cream, at LIPA (the Liverpool Institute of Performing Arts), Liverpool is preparing for the future.

In reality, is there enough between Liverpool and Manchester to make a world-class region? In simple audit terms the answer has to be yes. The raw material is there. Manchester has muscle and ambition. Liverpool has reputation and potential. Combined with the historic, rural, suburban and industrial attractions of Cumbria, Cheshire and Lancashire, the two cities should be able to

work together to compete with other countries, not just regions. Ireland, Denmark, Luxembourg, Belgium, the Balkans are inferior in simple GDP (Gross Domestic Product) terms. But it is not so much a matter of size, as of government.

English devolution proceeds at a gentle pace but meantime there are matters for the region itself to address. Impediments, some of its own making, must be cleared away. The secret is working together. The two conurbations almost touch each other. Some of the rivalries are absurd. For instance, we have two international airports and some people propound the fiction that they compete. Manchester Airport is an important hub with world reach. Liverpool Airport has developed apace as a low-cost regional facility, important in its own way, but it is not, and never will be, on a par with Manchester Airport. Together, however, they offer the region excellent options. For Merseyside to get the full benefit from Manchester Airport it should be promoting a direct high-speed rail link to it from Liverpool city centre.

In higher education, tourism, culture and sport, the drive must be towards more co-operation and integration. The universities must maximise opportunities to work together; offering identical,

Above Prime Minister Ramsay MacDonald laid the foundation stone for Manchester Central Library in 1930, and it was finally opened by King George V in 1934. The 'Architect and Building News' wrote: 'The Manchester Library is of international importance. In arrangement it resembles no other building of its kind.' At the time it was the largest public library in the country and it is still one of the busiest.

Opposite The Walker is now described as the 'National Gallery of the North'. Certainly, any visitor walking through the Corinthian pilasters towering above the building's entrance can look forward to an artistic feast inside the newly restored galleries. The Walker boasts one of the principal art collections in the country.

99

Right and below Tom Bloxham's Urban Splash company led the way in converting redundant buildings into highly desirable, new living space, drawing people back into the inner city. Here, the old Collegiate School building in Liverpool has been imaginatively transformed into a stunning residential complex.

Left Trendy apartments such as this one are springing up in the unlikeliest places: disused warehouses, factories, schools and office blocks. Brownfield sites are also being used to build prestigious new apartment blocks. One recent such project, close to Liverpool's Albert Dock, saw prospective buyers camping overnight to be first in the queue when the flats went on sale the next morning.

under-resourced and in some cases below-standard courses, is futile. The signs now are good. The loss of the synchrotron facility at Daresbury to the south was a painful wake-up call which municipal leaders and vice-chancellors heard. The formal concordat between the two cities, while it only produced a muted public response, was an important first step.

Each city has an acceptable tourist product. Together, especially with the added attractions of the three shires, it could be sensational. A cruise liner terminal on the Liverpool waterfront, bringing high-quality passenger shipping back to the Mersey, would be a massive boost to tourism in the whole North West, with visits offered to the Lake District, Blackpool, Chester and Manchester, as well as Liverpool itself. As the world population ages, Liverpool and Manchester are well placed to benefit from the twin growth areas of cruising and cultural tourism. But we must

be honest about our weather! We do enjoy the occasional glorious, still, warm days, but for much of the year we are obliged to offer visitors an indoor experience, with warmth and comfort guaranteed.

In culture and sport the secret is to offer complementary attractions. The distance between the cities is so short that audiences can easily travel between them. The age-old tradition that people from Manchester do not visit Liverpool and vice versa is finally breaking down and will accelerate with proper marketing and information exchange.

Perhaps the greatest challenge for the future is psychological. It has to be faced first and foremost by Liverpool. Manchester should be recognised by all as the region's capital city. Liverpool's compensation is its majestic history and heritage, its waterfront, the Beatles and its world role in popular culture and sport – a combination that makes it the region's irresistible tourism centre. Manchester's overall size, its geographical position, its commercial power and its financial muscle, put it ahead of Liverpool, but it is no region on its own. Should Manchester join hands with a rejuvenated Liverpool, a new force would be created. That, backed by the three strong counties of Lancashire, Cheshire and Cumbria, will once again make the North West a region to be reckoned with.

Above As the new Liverpool John Lennon Airport goes from strength to strength, and its terminal building reaches the final stages of a massive expansion and overhaul, its old terminal building has undergone a dramatic metamorphosis. The Grade II listed building is now a smart, four-star hotel, with all its original Art Deco features intact and faithfully restored. An upmarket gym with indoor and outdoor swimming pools and tennis courts now occupies an adjacent aircraft hangar.

Opposite The Old Wellington Inn (circa 1552) and the adjoining Sinclairs Oyster Bar are two of Manchester's oldest hostelries. They were sited originally in Shambles Square but were dismantled during reconstruction of the city centre following the IRA bomb attack in 1996 and re-erected with many of their original timbers in Manchester's mediaeval quarter.

103

Right Opened in 1965 as the University Theatre, the newly refurbished Contact Theatre retains its close relationship with the University of Manchester's Drama Department. The Contact company has always been dedicated to the needs of young people, and through its workshops and productions it is able to reach out to groups who would not normally have access to such facilities.

Right below Built on the Salford docks with grants from the public and private sector, including a £127m grant from the National Lottery, the Lowry forms the magnificent centrepiece of Salford Quays. The building includes two theatres, three art galleries and the largest collection of Lowry paintings in the world.

Opposite Tate Liverpool is the largest gallery of modern and contemporary art outside London. A stylishly converted warehouse in the Albert Dock, the Tate houses two types of exhibit: art selected from the Tate collection and special exhibitions of contemporary art. The clear, cool light of its riverside location suffuses the building, enhancing the works on display.

Opposite below The Royal Exchange Theatre is a building within a building. Housed inside the huge trading hall of the once mighty Royal Exchange (which controlled 80 per cent of the world trade in finished cloth), the theatre is like a lunar module; a startling and exciting high-tech reinterpretation of an important building.

Right Old Trafford football ground, Manchester – 'Theatre of Dreams' and home to the incomparable Manchester United, Premier League Champions on numerous occasions.

Right below Treble-winning heroes of Liverpool Football Club, parading their unique collection of three Cup trophies in 2001. Liverpool has won more trophies than any other English club.

Left Old Trafford cricket ground, Manchester, home to Lancashire County Cricket Club and one of England's regular Test match grounds. It was here, in 1956, that Jim Laker performed the extraordinary feat of taking 19 wickets in a Test against Australia.

Left below The Grand National, run each April at Aintree on the outskirts of Liverpool, is the most demanding and longest of all steeplechases. It now enjoys the largest worldwide television audience of any single annual sporting event. A fine statue commemorates the feat of Red Rum, trained locally by Ginger McCain, in winning the race three times.

Right The importance of the square in city life, so obvious in most European cities, has at last been recognised in this country. In both Liverpool and Manchester, the square has been 'reinvented', with old squares being revitalised and new squares created. They can be vibrant meeting places crammed with cafés, restaurants and live music, or peaceful green spaces in which to read, picnic, wander, or simply sit and enjoy the sunshine.

Left Developments in urban design are making the region's cities more user-friendly, illustrated by the impressive Trinity Bridge (above), which links Salford to Manchester's city centre, and the futuristic Corporation Street footbridge (below).

Right and opposite The natural exuberance of the North West finds expression in a huge variety of popular festivals. The annual calendar is crammed with communal celebrations ranging from small-scale village fêtes, to city carnivals attracting thousands of visitors to the region each year.

famous lives

Martin Wainwright

'It is often interesting, although not invariably so, to read a man's verdict on himself.
What is still more interesting is the verdict of others upon him.' Lord Jenkins of Hillhead

Picture a dinner party to which Beatrix Potter, the Duke of Bridgewater, John Bright, the Beatles, Tom Bloxham, David Beckham and Beryl Bainbridge have been invited and then imagine how each would enliven the evening with his or her different speciality. Conversation would surely flow, with topics ranging from canal construction to musical lyrics, literary criticism to urban vision, or anthropomorphic rabbits to famous goals. Such an array of diverse talents, but each sharing a common heritage of having made their name in England's North West.

Perhaps it is inevitable that so many square miles of Britain should produce such a rich crop of brilliant citizens, but few regions can match the procession of inventiveness and talent which has flowered between the rolling plains of Cheshire and the bleak landscape of Hadrian's Wall. From here came William Gladstone and Sir Robert Peel, two of Britain's greatest Prime Ministers. From here came Henry Tate, benefactor of one of the most dynamic art galleries in the world, Lord Norman Foster, architect of some of the most stunning buildings and Sir John Barbirolli, conductor of a long succession of memorable orchestral concerts.

Major movements in the affairs of mankind have also been launched in the North West by North Westerners. John Bright, and his political mentor Richard Cobden, were the apostles of world-wide free trade, providing the dynamo for the burgeoning economies of nineteenth century Europe and America. John Kay with his flying shuttle, Robert Owen, creator of the model factory system, and the Duke of Bridgewater, canal pioneer, spearheaded a corps of North Western inventors and entrepreneurs, who firmly established the Industrial Revolution in the sheltered valleys nestling between the sheep-grazed Pennine moors.

Three North Western virtues have repeatedly nurtured such talent, each of them drawn from the landscape and history of England's north western seaboard. Each achiever has thrived in a context which encourages dogged persistence and hard work. Each has absorbed aspects of often magical surroundings, from Scafell Pike to Alderley Edge. Above all, each has learned to reach out – to the rest of Britain, to the four corners of the world, and even, through the telescopes of Sir Bernard Lovell at Jodrell Bank, to the limitless stars in the universe.

This all may sound lyrical, but who established the word 'lyrical' more firmly in the language of English literature than that great North Westerner, William Wordsworth? His most famous collection of poetry, whose very title was *Lyrical Ballads*, draws heavily on the physically powerful landscape of his youth. The hiss of skates on a Lakeland tarn, in a

Opposite Eric Bartholomew would be amused by this tribute to one of Britain's greatest comedians. Known to all as Eric Morecambe, his famous pose, captured in bronze, is proving a major attraction to the seaside resort he loved so much that he took its name.

113

Right Toad Lane, Rochdale, marks the place where the Co-operative movement began. Local workers were angered by mill owners who controlled the local shops and determined their high prices. Forming the Rochdale Equitable Pioneers Society, they set in motion a workers' movement that was to sweep the world.

Opposite Enterprise and leadership. A new generation of successful entrepreneurs, personified by Meera Pathak, Shami Ahmed and Tom Bloxham, continue the region's strong tradition of creative enterprise, previously epitomised by the likes of John Moores, founder of Littlewoods and arts benefactor. Inspired leadership of the kind displayed by Gerald, 6th Duke of Westminster, and University Chancellors Anna Ford and Cherie Booth, contribute to a strong sense of regional identity, whilst the vision of Manchester University's computer pioneer Tom Kilburn and the success of ethical banking as instigated by Terry Thomas and developed by The Co-operative Bank have placed the North West at the forefront of modern business methods.

landscape exquisitely outlined with sparkling hoar-frost, is echoed in his verses, as are the bleak, blustery fell tops and quaint cobbled streets of his native Cockermouth. Wordsworth is also notorious for the banality of his worst verse and, to a degree, so too are the humble instruments of North Western life; and that too is significant. The laureate called a spade a spade, literally. One of his lesser-recited odes begins: 'Spade! With which Wilkinson hath tilled his lands!' It is this combination of inspired creativity, overlaying the most mundane, everyday detail, which also fired the imagination of his most celebrated modern successors, the Liverpool Poets.

While the Beatles were writing lyrics for their performances in the Cavern, revealing a keen awareness of their home surroundings in songs like *Penny Lane* and *Strawberry Fields* — Adrian Henry, Brian Patten and Roger McGough turned such unlikely subjects as buses, the East Lancashire Road and even the Mersey Ferry Pier, into memorable verse. Across the world, from Haight Astbury in San Francisco, to Moscow's Arbat Street, poems like McGough's *At Lunchtime* and *A Story of Love*, in which extraordinary things happen on a Liverpool bus, were chanted as mantras of the 1960s. In poetry clubs and pub readings internationally, they still are.

Always conscious of Wordsworth's mantle, the Liverpool Poets have also always acknowledged the influence of their North West predecessor, Wilfred Owen, who conveyed the agonies of the Western Front with such terrible pathos. In prose, however, the torch was carried on after Wordsworth by Elizabeth Gaskell, always known cosily as 'Mrs Gaskell', the dutiful wife of Reverend William, whose Unitarian chapel in Cross Street, Manchester, was the founding place of the *Manchester Guardian* and a beacon for radicalism all over the

Meena Pathak, ethnic food entrepreneur.

Duke of Westminster, landowner and businessman.

Lord Terry Thomas, ethical banker.

Cherie Booth, Chancellor, Liverpool JM University.

Sir John Moores, businessman.

Professor Tom Kilburn, computer pioneer.

Shami Ahmed, entrepreneur.

Anna Ford, Chancellor, University of Manchester.

Tom Bloxham, urban regeneration visionary.

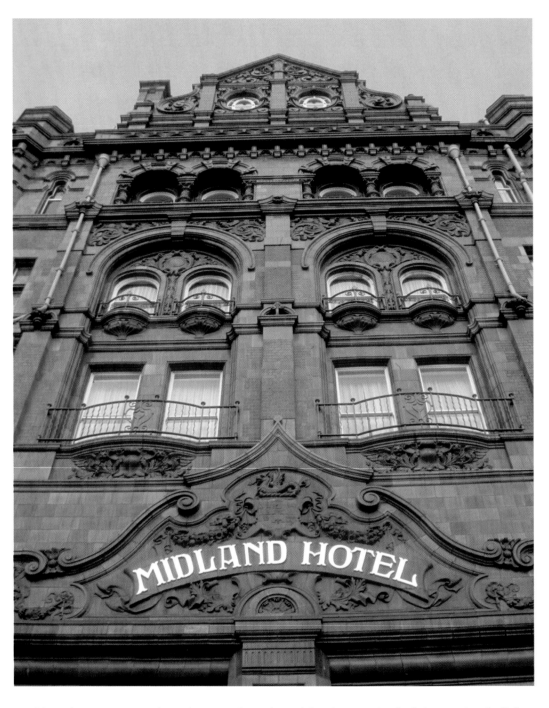

Right Charles Trubshaw's lavish Midland Hotel was the meeting place for two entrepreneurs whose vision was equally extravagant: to build the best car in the world. The result of Charles Rolls meeting Henry Royce in May 1904, was the Rolls Royce, a car which has always symbolised quality and engineering excellence.

world. In her writing, such as her novel *North and South*, Mrs Gaskell 'out-radicalled' her husband, taking the part of the downtrodden workers of mid-nineteenth century Britain with such eloquence, that even the *Manchester Guardian* accused her of 'excessively maligning' all Manchester manufacturers.

Mrs Gaskell was not in the least deterred by such criticism, any more than was the suffragette leader, Emmeline Pankhurst, who grew up in the next generation of Mancunians and was unstoppable in her fight for women's political rights. Some years later, the practical-

Above and left William Hesketh Lever is one of many pivotal figures to have changed the face of the region. A remarkable industrialist and philanthropist, Lever sited his Sunlight Soap works on greenfield land near Birkenhead. A man of great compassion, Lever commissioned top architects to design a housing estate for his workers next to the factory. Port Sunlight village was beautifully landscaped with every amenity for his workers, including the Lady Lever Art Gallery, a memorial to his wife, and now part of the National Museums and Galleries on Merseyside.

minded North Westerner, Marie Stopes, continued this feminist tradition when she pioneered birth control, probably the single biggest factor in women's liberation. In the twentieth century the feisty novelist, Beryl Bainbridge, took up the torch. She is a writer who has not so much left her native Liverpool as taken it with her to London, as a source of inspiration and strong social feeling, in book after successful book. In the same way, Anthony Burgess, prolific author of the highest rank, will never forget his Catholic upbringing in inner Manchester.

Right Carr House at Much Hoole, near Preston, where astronomer Jeremiah Horrocks plotted the transit of Venus. Horrocks, a farmer's son born in Toxteth, Liverpool in 1619, was regarded by Isaac Newton as a genius. At the age of thirteen, he entered Emmanuel College, Cambridge as a 'sizar' or poor scholar and taught himself astronomy. Returning to Toxteth, he used Kepler's Law of Planetary Motion to prove that the Moon orbited the Earth elliptically. His greatest breakthrough was to observe the transit of Venus, proving that the planets revolved round the Sun and not the Earth. Tragically, Horrocks died suddenly at the age of 23, having transformed the science of astronomy.

John, Paul, George and Ringo famously held onto their birthright, too. Even today, Sir Paul McCartney's voice – like that of his fellow Liverpudlian Cilla Black – retains its Liverpool twang, that touch of the Irish which also lies in the magical feyness of Lennon-McCartney songs. The Beatles moved on to celebrate the very different virtues of New York and Scotland's fogbound Mull of Kintyre, but they always acknowledged the Mersey water flowing through their veins. Sir Paul's school for his talented young successors on Merseyside, the Liverpool Institute for Performing Arts, is one of the city's modern attractions.

The 'Fab Four' were by no means the inventors of this loyalty to their humble backstreets. Gracie Fields of Rochdale got there first. Her songs were drawn from the cobbled streets and alleyways of the steep-streeted Pennine town, evoking the clatter of mill girls' clogs, as the hooters wailed out the beginning and end of shifts in the mills. She made a lot of money and eventually retired to the Italian island of Capri, but she always remained 'Our Gracie', and her voice is still a powerful emblem of the North West, many years after her death.

Our Gracie was also symbolic of an innocent, picturebook world, in which decent girls overcame the obstacles of poverty. The sort of girls who might have taken a tram to Port Sunlight on their afternoon off – a monument to another genius of the region,

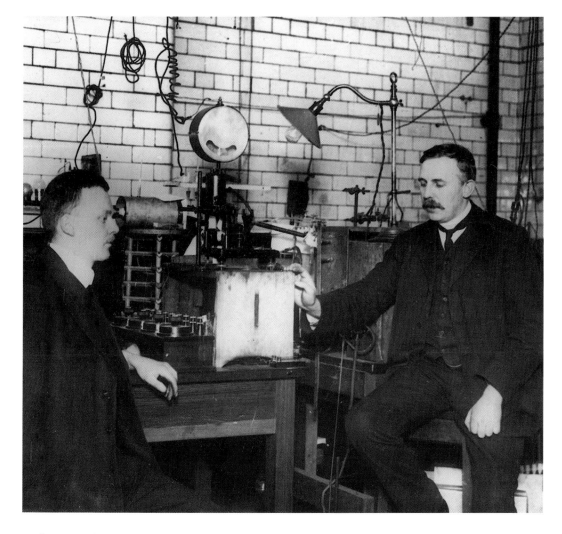

William Hesketh Lever, the first Lord Leverhulme, whose enormously prosperous businesses were in large part also missionary work. Like the Scott family of the *Manchester Guardian*, who sacrificed a personal fortune to hand over the ownership of the newspaper to an unimpeachably independent trust, Leverhulme's interests stretched way beyond soap manufacture and making money and he worked hard to develop his own brand of benevolent paternalism. He was not so much inspired by the North West's landscape, like the poets and novelists, as determined to change it for the better. And in Port Sunlight, he did just that.

His ambitions and funding for a model community in Wirral, close to the lawns and shrubberies of Birkenhead Park, from which New York's Central Park took inspiration, drew the best landscape planners and architects to the North West. In the process, Leverhulme transformed the architecture department of Liverpool University into the most exciting and forward-looking in Britain. The greatest and brightest, from Norman Shaw to Charles Reilly, combined to design picturesque cottages for soap-making workers, many of them satisfyingly funded by a huge libel settlement paid to Lord Leverhulme by the *Daily Mail*, which had falsely accused Lever Brothers of running a cartel.

William Roache, actor.

Gracie Fields, singer and film star.

Beryl Bainbridge, writer.

Heather Small, singer.

LS Lowry, painter.

Sir Ben Kingsley, actor.

Lord Melvyn Bragg, writer and television presenter.

Sir Tom Courtenay, actor.

Sir Paul McCartney, musician.

120

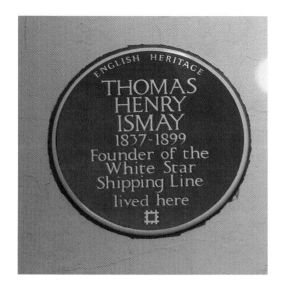

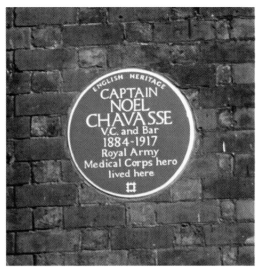

The greatest town-planner of the twentieth century, Sir Patrick Abercrombie, grew up in this stimulating North West renaissance, just as the architect of the Natural History Museum and Manchester Town Hall, Alfred Waterhouse, had done half a century earlier. And a similar sense of excitement animates their and Lord Leverhulme's successor today; Tom Bloxham, the Liverpool-based wizard in charge of something almost inconceivable: a wholly new North West landscape. A lateral thinker, Bloxham had the simple idea one day of looking upwards, instead of down at his feet. What he saw was millions of square feet of unused roof space.

The result was Bloxham's 'Loft Revolution', the reinvention of central Liverpool and Manchester as places in which to live; not just any old place, but *the* place, with fashionable restaurants and pavement cafés like Barcelona or Paris, all-night clubs, private gyms and attractive open spaces in which to wander, such as the restored towpaths of the cities' canals. Bloxham called his company Urban Splash, and a splash is what it made. His first, pioneering apartments have been joined by thousands of others, as well as flagship city centre buildings such as Trafford's Imperial War Museum North, Salford's stunning Lowry and Manchester's sleek, glass-sheathed Urbis.

For all these architects and planners, their policy was to aim high and look up – following in the footsteps of earlier North Western innovators such as Henry Royce, whose engines now power the aircraft of the world; his neighbour, Sir AV Roe, whose Avro company built the Lancaster bomber, stalwart of the Second World War; and of Alcock and Brown, another local pair, who used an early Avro to make the first flight across the Atlantic.

Inevitably, the glitter of these multi-million pound projects and the new urban gentry who can pay hundreds of thousands of pounds for a loft apartment, present a stark contrast to the poverty which still afflicts other parts of the North West. This will not disappear through simple statistics such as the fact that the Salford Quays offices and shops round the Lowry now employ more people than the old, vanished docks. But there should be no pretence; Walter Greenwood's great classic of urban poverty, *Love on the Dole*, established another particular genius of the North West: the ability to discover and describe the region's

Opposite Creative and cultural genius; stars of stage and screen. Paul McCartney's enduring musical talent, Beryl Bainbridge's acutely-observed novels, Ben Kingsley's film portrayal of leading characters and Melvyn Bragg's distinctive broadcasting style demonstrate the range of the North West cultural talent; whilst William Roache who plays Ken Barlow in Granada Television's 'Coronation Street', pop-star Heather Small and Liverpool-born conductor Simon Rattle, have followed in the popular and artistic footsteps of Rochdale's Gracie Fields and Salford's LS Lowry.

Left English Heritage have recently extended their Blue Plaque scheme outside of London, with Merseyside the first area to have been selected. Nominated by the public, the first fourteen plaques are an eclectic mix:

SIR PATRICK ABERCROMBIE (1879-1957) pioneering town planner.

BESSIE BRADDOCK (1899-1970) Labour politician and campaigner.

JOHN BRODIE (1858-1934) City Engineer.

CAPTAIN NOEL CHAVASSE, VC and Bar (1884-1917) war hero.

PETER ELLIS (1804-1884) architect.

FRANK HORNBY (1863-1936) toy manufacturer (Meccano).

THOMAS HENRY ISMAY (1837-1899) founder of the White Star Line.

JOHN LENNON (1940-1980), musician and songwriter.

JOSEPH MAYER (1803-1886) antiquary and collector.

WILFRED OWEN (1893-1918) war poet.

WILLIAM RATHBONE (1819-1902) and ELEANOR RATHBONE (1872-1946) social reformers.

SIR CHARLES REILLY (1874-1948) Professor of Architecture.

SIR RONALD ROSS (1857-1932) discoverer of the mosquito transmission of malaria.

SIR HENRY TATE (1819-1899) sugar magnate and founder of the Tate Gallery.

Right Statue of Alan Turing in Sackville Street, Manchester. Turing was one of the great pioneers of the computer. As a mathematician, he applied the concept of the algorithm to digital computers. His research into the relationship between machines and nature created the field of artificial intelligence. He is best known to a wider public for his work in breaking the computer code used by the Germans in their Enigma machine. After the war, he worked at the University of Manchester on the development of the Manchester Automatic Digital Machine (MADAM), believing that by the year 2000 machines would be able to replicate human minds. Sadly, he never lived to see the development of the computer age, dying in 1954.

Opposite The Lewis Carroll window in All Saints Church, Daresbury. Another mathematician, Charles Dodgson, is regarded as a genius but in a totally different sphere. Born the son of the local vicar in Daresbury, a small village near Warrington, Charles spent his early formative years roaming the neighbourhood. These influences surfaced later in his two great works, 'Alice in Wonderland' and 'Alice Through the Looking Glass', written under the pseudonym Lewis Carroll.

downside honestly and unflinchingly, and present that, as well as the successes, to the wider world. Greenwood's picture was all the more convincing because it did not deny its struggling heroes and heroines all pleasure. In the book, the young lovers take a memorable trip from Salford to the softly rural North Lancashire coast, where, in a brief interlude from their daily grind, they listen, entranced, to music from the bandstand in the park.

Music – yet another field of North Western genius which has been a countervailing leveller of social distinctions, and a real engine of democracy. This is the world of Barbirolli, the Liverpool Philharmonic (affectionately known as the 'Phil'), Sir Malcolm Sargent and the glorious Hallé Orchestra; the latter, reported a hundred years ago by the inimitable Neville

Right Liverpool-born legend, Simon Rattle, is currently Artistic Director and Principal Conductor of the Berlin Philharmonic Orchestra. Although still only in his forties, he has received a huge number of prestigious awards, honorary doctorates and a knighthood, each bearing testimony to his brilliant musical career.

Opposite Perhaps the twentieth century's most famous faces, The Beatles are recognised and adored by millions across the entire globe. These four Liverpool lads rewrote the history of popular music and heralded in a worldwide cultural revolution.

Cardus of the *Guardian*, now rings out in the Bridgewater Hall under the baton of Mark Elder. Such top quality music is available to everyone, even those on low incomes, as discounted tickets are on offer for all performances.

Could the might of the magnificent Hallé drown out that other great sound of North Western heroes – the roar of the football crowds at Old Trafford, or the legendary Anfield Kop? Like the Grand National racecourse at Aintree, these have been like Roman arenas for generation after generation of extraordinary sporting geniuses. There is something eminently North Western in the two remarkable figures who manage the teams today: Sir Alex Ferguson and Gerard Houllier. Their accents may be Scottish or French, as are their origins, but, in the tradition of Liverpool's immortal Bill Shankly and Manchester United's Sir Matt Busby, they have shown that the man in the suit (and tracksuit) behind the scenes can be more crucial to success than any of the glamorous stars.

Above Football is the region's passion and it is fitting that its great sporting heroes are permanently recognised. Dixie Dean, of Everton, was one of the greatest centre-forwards of all time – it is unlikely that any player will ever surpass his record of 60 League goals in the 1927/28 season. Sir Matt Busby was revered by followers of Manchester United in the same way that his close friend Bill Shankly was adored by the Anfield faithful of Liverpool Football Club.

Opposite David Beckham and Michael Owen are just the latest in a succession of world-class superstars representing North West sport. The pace of Wigan rugby league star Billy Boston, the dedication of Hoylake cyclist Chris Boardman and the defiance of cricketer Michael Atherton, brought them to the very pinnacle of their respective sports, whilst the great West Indian batsman Clive Lloyd chose to settle in the region, leading Lancashire to national Cup triumphs. Cumbrian Chris Bonington has led successful Everest and other major expeditions, whilst equine courage in like measure brought Red Rum, trained in the region by Ginger McCain, three famous victories over the 30 formidable fences of Aintree's Grand National. But for all-round sporting excellence, none can compare with Wirral-born Lottie Dod, five times Wimbledon champion, Olympic archery medallist, British Ladies golf champion, ice-skater and mountaineer.

But it is high time to take our seats for dinner; look how many extra places we have had to fit in. Exceptional footballers like Sir Bobby Charlton, Sir Tom Finney and Sir Stanley Matthews; cricketers Cyril Washbrook and Brian Statham of Lancashire and England, Clive Lloyd of Lancashire and the West Indies. Successful actors such as Albert Finney, John Thaw and Ben Kingsley, actress turned politician Glenda Jackson, journalist and broadcaster Alastair Cooke, artist LS Lowry, whose Salford street scenes captured a whole way of life, Stan Laurel and his successor Eric Morecambe who forever performs the Sunshine Dance in Graham Ibbeson's inspired statue on Morecambe Prom, George Formby and Arthur Askey. Also here is Alan Turing, whose genius led to our laptops and modems, and his fellow Cambridge scientific genius Lord Rutherford, who split the atom; John Moores of the wealth-spreading Littlewoods Pools; Cherie Blair, actor's daughter from Liverpool, Queen's Counsel and Prime Minister's wife, Anna Ford; TV personality and vicar's daughter from the Lake District, who is now Chancellor of Manchester University; Lord Carman, the fox of the English bar.

And JRR Tolkien is here too, as an inky schoolboy from Stoneyhurst College, no doubt getting on famously with John Dalton, the father of modern chemistry, who isolated marsh gas from the ponds around early nineteenth century Manchester, and John Ruskin, the great critic and democratiser of High Art, who retired to brood in the Lakes. Like the road to adventure in the song which the Elves of Rivendell sing in *The Lord of the Rings*, the list of potential outstanding North Western guests '… goes ever on and on …'

Billy Boston, Wigan and England.

Sir Chris Bonington, mountaineer.

Chris Boardman, Olympic cycling champion.

Michael Owen, Liverpool and England.

Clive Lloyd, Lancashire and West Indies.

David Beckham, Manchester United and England.

Lottie Dod, Britain's finest all-round sportswoman.

Mike Atherton, Lancashire and England.

Red Rum and trainer Ginger McCain.

prosperity built on knowledge

John Pickstone

*'For the first time in recorded history
the survival of the country depends upon the universities.' Lord Bowden of Chesterfield*

The North West led the burgeoning of the world's first Industrial Revolution and then pioneered global trade in industrial products. The textile business has declined, but companies once built on dyestuffs are now world leaders in pharmaceuticals. The engineering talents once focused on looms and steam-locomotives are now turned to aerospace; local electrical firms and radar know-how from the Second World War has helped Britain build its computer industry.

Industrial innovation is mobile; geographies of trade change over decades, and success requires constant change. But traditions of creativity can be built up, and engines of innovation created for one purpose can be turned to others, as the North West abundantly shows. Pride in history is not the enemy of invention. In the North West, invention is the very core of history.

At first sight, the Lake District would seem to be the very opposite of technical. Was it not the home of poets rather than scientists? Indeed, and those poets still draw the crowds, but look around Coniston or Keswick and see also the traces of the metal mining which brought a prosperity and practicality which pre-dated the Romantic poets. In the later eighteenth century, the trades of the region were often in the hands of Quakers – men of simple faith and a strong educational tradition. Several pioneering doctors came from the region, and several scientists who provided leadership in Cambridge and London. One of them, William Whewell, actually invented the word 'scientist'.

In the 1780s a young teacher from Kendal came south to Manchester to join a new college set up by ministers, doctors and merchants. Each summer John Dalton returned to the Lakes; but the rest of his days were spent in his Manchester laboratory with his private pupils. When he died in 1844, he was the patron saint of Manchester science, known world-wide for his atomic theory of the chemical elements, and a hero to manufacturers and working-men. His statue in Manchester Town Hall's entrance faces that of his pupil James Prescott Joule, whose name is now known everywhere for his work on energy. Joule ran the family brewery – and carried out experiments at home.

But it was not just scientists who had made cotton manufacturing into a global industry; it was entrepreneurs who used the inventions of artisans. John Kay invented the 'flying shuttle' which allowed the hand-weaving of wider cloths; James Hargreaves of Blackburn devised the 'jenny' on which several threads could be spun simultaneously; Richard Arkwright of Preston developed the 'water frame' which used rollers to draw out the threads; and Samuel Crompton of Bolton combined the actions of the jenny and the water-frame into the 'mule' – the basis for the massive spinning machines developed through the nineteenth century. Arkwright made lots of money by putting spinning machines into the factories he built; but Crompton died a poor man.

Opposite A familiar and strangely mysterious night-time scene at the Castner Kellner plant at Runcorn, one of the region's enduring industrial landmarks. The former ICI plant, now owned by Belgian-based Ineos Chlor, produces the bulk of Britain's chlorine supplies. There has been a chemical works on the site for over 100 years.

129

Above Pilkington's world leading glass manufacturing plant at St Helens. The company has been a pioneer in the global glass industry for over 100 years. Its latest invention is a self-cleaning glass which virtually eliminates the chore of window cleaning. The key element is a special chemical coating, equivalent in thickness to a penny coin on top of the Empire State Building.

Opposite Among the great feats of nineteenth century engineering, the building of the Manchester Ship Canal demands particular attention. A much greater engineering achievement than the Suez Canal, over 16,000 navvies shovelled their way from Eastham, in Wirral, to Manchester. The canal connected the city directly to world markets for the first time and soon the Port of Manchester was the third largest in the country, after London and Liverpool, despite being 40 miles from the sea.

At first the factories were alongside the soft-water Pennine streams; from about 1800, pioneering canals and steam engines allowed mills to be built in towns, where labour was more readily available. By 1900, some Lancashire towns had more cotton looms than people. At its peak, Oldham had 17 million spindles in 300 mills.

Manchester had grown as a trading centre for hand-crafted textiles. From about 1780 factories appeared in the district, and from about 1800 in the vicinity of the town. You can see them still, by the Rochdale Canal in Ancoats, perhaps the world's first industrial suburb. They were built by merchants and engineers, many of them Scottish, who discovered how to run huge mechanical factories and who invented, for better or worse, the science of management. They pioneered the world's first passenger railway between Liverpool and Manchester, and invented the weekend — when Saturday afternoon became a holiday. It was a Scottish chemist in Manchester who developed the Mackintosh to repel the rain.

Most of the cotton was exported, and the shipping trade depended on Liverpool — one of the world's greatest ports from the eighteenth century. It was close to the chemical industries which exploited Lancashire coal and Cheshire salt. Around Runcorn and Widnes, along the River Mersey and the Bridgewater Canal, chemical manufacturing thrived. Much of what became ICI was created here, as was much of the soap manufacturing which floated Unilever. At St Helens, Pilkington developed the glass-making techniques which still dominate the industry.

Right Bentley Motors at Crewe, Cheshire, is undergoing unprecedented expansion by new owners Volkswagen AG. A key element of their £500m investment programme will be a new mid-size GT coupé which will help to raise production from 1,800 units a year to 9,000. In 2001 Bentley made a triumphant return to Le Mans.

Right below Avecia, Europe's largest privately owned specialty chemicals company at Blackley, Manchester, employs state-of-the-art robotic testing equipment to analyse inkjet colourants. A world leader in many areas of specialty chemicals production, the company holds over 30 Queen's Awards for export, innovation and the environment.

Before about 1850, formal higher education rarely featured in such stories; thereafter its significance increased. The region benefited from the immigration of German engineers and chemists such as Charles Beyer (of Beyer-Peacock locomotives), and Ludwig Mond of Brunner Mond. They worked alongside local engineers trained by apprenticeship, such as Joseph Whitworth who developed precision gauges, standard screws, accurate plane surfaces and guns.

Whitworth left a huge legacy for the benefit of Manchester – art, science, medicine, and its municipal technical school (now UMIST), built around 1900 to rival the German polytechnics. Though institutes for the education of factory and shop workers date from the 1820s, secular education above school level was not public until the 1850s, when Owens College was founded in Manchester from the legacy of a local merchant. The market for higher education was initially uncertain, but by the 1870s Owens had new Gothic buildings in a pleasant suburb, and by the 1880s the federal Victoria University had been established to include Leeds and Liverpool. It employed some notable scholars and one of the creators of modern economics, WS Jevons, but its most famous staff were scientists and engineers. By the start of the twentieth century, Manchester

Right AstraZeneca's research and development campus at Alderley Park, Cheshire, where 2,700 scientists and technicians lead the fight against cancer, cardio-vascular disease, inflammation and infection. It was here that Tamoxifen was discovered and developed 30 years ago. The drug, the most commonly prescribed treatment for breast cancer, has prolonged the lives of 400,000 women around the world.

had one of the finest chemical laboratories in the world and a new physics institute headed by Ernest Rutherford, along with another Nobel-prize winner, Niels Bohr. Osborne Reynolds (of Reynolds numbers) was Professor of Engineering, and at one stage the philosopher Ludwig Wittgenstein was a research student, flying meteorological balloons on the moors above Glossop.

Liverpool University developed rapidly, aided by the ship-owners who ran the city. Science departments were closely linked to the city's commercial interests – from the chemistry of the food trades to the tropical medicine required to open up Africa for imperial agriculture and settlement. Pharmaceutical companies, notably Evans, developed alongside the university. Charles Sherrington, one of the Edwardian founders of the neurosciences, did his best work at Liverpool, which also had the country's first chair in biochemistry, paid for by brewing barons. Ronald Ross won the Nobel Prize for his work on malaria.

Soon after the First World War the cotton industry entered a long decline, threatening to undermine the economy of the region. The smaller manufacturing towns suffered much, but the cities were better buffered and remained creative. American links replaced those with Germany. Westinghouse had been established in the new industrial estate of Trafford Park in 1902; it gave rise to Metro Vickers, a national leader in advanced electrical engineering, working closely with the universities. Also at Trafford Park, Henry Ford in 1911 opened his first European plant, to manufacture the Model T; and new petroleum plants and food technologies, like Kellogs, often had American links. In north Manchester, the ICI Dyestuffs division consolidated local fine-chemical companies, whilst heavy chemicals in South East Lancashire were rationalised into another division of ICI.

Left The computer games industry has taken strong root in the North West, attracting the attention of global players. Two of the market's popular games – 'Wipeout Fusion' and 'Formula 1, 2001' – have been developed in Liverpool by the former small games publisher Psygnosis, which is now part of Sony Computer Entertainment Europe. The group employs nearly 300 designers, programmers, artists and support staff at the Wavertree Technology Park, developing games for Playstation 2, some of which are sold in Japan and America.

Left below Oldham's historical association with Ferranti has left the town with a legacy of world-beating technologies. Semi-conductors is one area where Chadderton-based Zetex is using its expertise to produce high performance transistor devices for use in automotives, data processing, communications, industrial and consumer products.

Right BAE SYSTEMS has a major design, manufacturing and flight-testing presence in the North West in a range of defence products including Eurofighter. The Warton and Samlesbury sites in Lancashire have felt the greatest benefit from investment over recent years.

On Eurofighter alone, over £350m has been invested since 1996 in leading-edge IT systems and manufacturing processes to introduce advanced manufacturing technologies and fundamentally change the way of working. Eurofighter has 100 per cent digital design along with digital manufacture and digital inspection.

Some fields of medicine became much more technical – especially radiotherapy. In the 1930s, Manchester's Christie Hospital became internationally known for systematised radium treatments of cancer. It had benefited from the university's eminence in radioactivity, and co-operated with Metro Vickers on the development of high voltage apparatus. The North West was also known for its orthopaedics, pioneered in Victorian Liverpool by a Welsh family of bone-setters, one of whom became a GP near the Liverpool docks. His nephew, Robert Jones, organised the fracture service for the digging of the massive Manchester Ship Canal in the 1890s, and then led the national fracture service during the First World War. His Manchester protégé, Harry Platt, developed civilian fracture clinics between the wars; and his protégé, John Charnley, established prostheses as an effective treatment for hip joints, thus laying the basis for much of the implant industry. All five generations were from the region, and worked here all their lives.

Aircraft factories were boosted to meet the Second World War effort – of which the Avro Lancaster Bomber was the most famous product – later forming a key part of what today is BAE SYSTEMS. Together with its suppliers, it forms a multi-billion pound defence-related industry, linked with the universities as the North West Aerospace Alliance. Jet engines were made by Joseph Lucas in Burnley and by Rolls Royce in Barnoldswick.

Left Good design of new workspace is a necessity, not an unaffordable luxury. The curvaceous Simon Jersey office and factory extension, Accrington, is an inspirational architectural showpiece influenced by energy conscious design. The company makes corporate wear.

Left below The architecture of the former Bryant and May match factory in Speke, Liverpool, has been updated to give the listed building a modern business feel. It is now occupied by 7C, a provider of outsourced call centres, an industry that has taken strong root in the region. When fully staffed, the building will employ more people than the match factory in its heyday.

Right The new Ruskin Library at the University of Lancaster houses important archive material, thus helping to preserve the region's past, whilst the clean modern lines of the building illustrate a determination to stay at the forefront of design and regeneration. Such investment is widespread and underlines the region's strong commitment to Higher Education.

The pharmaceuticals industry, too, was boosted by the war-time collaborations to make penicillin; Glaxo developed its antibiotic fermentation plant at Ulverston; and at Speke, near Liverpool, Distillers and Eli Lilly were to develop biotechnologies for antibiotics, insulin and human growth hormone. ICI entered pharmaceuticals seriously after the war, first in its Dyestuffs Division in North Manchester, then from the 1970s in a new research centre at Alderley Park, in Cheshire, now owned by the world-leading AstraZeneca. ICI also used its war-time expertise to develop new anaesthetics based on fluorine chemistry from the atomic bomb project; James Black developed beta blockers for the treatment of hypertension.

Much of the post-war nuclear power industry was concentrated in the North West. Risley became the HQ of the Industrial Division of the Atomic Energy Authority, and Calder Hall in Cumberland became Britain's first atomic power station. It was followed by the nuclear waste reprocessing complex Sellafield, where a £100m technology centre opened in 2001. A large linear accelerator was built at Daresbury as part of the National Institute for Research in Nuclear

Science. Manchester University studies on cosmic rays and war-time work on radar led to Bernard Lovell's elegant radio-telescope at Jodrell Bank, which became instantly world-famous for tracking the Sputnik and remains a landmark of rural Cheshire. Also at Manchester University, Freddie Williams and Tom Kilburn developed the first electronic stored-program computer in 1948, while the logician Alan Turing wrote one of the first programs.

Collaboration with Ferranti established the North West as a leader in the British computer industry. Vivian Bowden, who had trained under Rutherford, worked for Ferranti and declared himself the world's first computer salesman. He then led UMIST through a period of major expansion, whilst also serving the Ministry of Technology in the mid 1960s. He also prompted the development at UMIST of a museum, which later moved to Castlefield, incorporated Liverpool Road Station – the world's earliest surviving passenger terminus – and became the Museum of Science and Industry.

These post-war technologies shaped much of British industry into the 1970s. Since then, the world of science and industry has revolved again; and again the North West has adapted to maintain leadership positions. There are now substantial universities in Lancaster, Preston and Salford, as well as three in Manchester and two in Liverpool. If proposals on the table can be agreed, then two of the Manchester institutions, UMIST and the University of Manchester, will merge to form a single new seat of learning, with 28,000 students and a turnover of half a billion pounds.

The Mersey valley remains a key site for chemicals and for the glass industry, which Pilkington continues to lead. Its latest innovation, self-cleaning glass, demonstrates how minute knowledge of surface chemistry can solve very practical problems. Avecia, one of the specialist chemical companies created out of ICI Dyestuffs, is a world-leader in oligo-nucleotides. Specialist textile firms remain an important part of the regional economy.

In the North West, as elsewhere, the biomedical sciences have become steadily more important. Since the 1980s UMIST has transformed its brewing research into bio-molecular engineering. Manchester University has established a faculty of biomedical sciences noted for molecular and cell biology, tissue engineering and studies of disease parasites. It works closely

with industry, with the medical school, and with several teaching hospitals. Manchester has a reputation for its successful medical collaboration – in the neurosciences at Hope Hospital, Salford, and on breast cancer, for which Christie Hospital, St Mary's, and South Manchester hospitals are internationally known. St Mary's, with Southampton, was recently recognised as a national centre for clinical genetics.

International pharmaceutical companies continue to develop major operations in the region, from Glaxo at Ulverston to Evans Vaccines near Liverpool. AstraZeneca at Alderley Park is now a major global research site, with over 2,700 scientists and technicians, concentrating on remedies for cancer, cardio-vascular disease, inflammation and infection. One of Alderley Park's great successes is the breast-cancer drug Tamoxifen, to which nearly 400,000 women now owe their lives. These academic and industrial strengths make the North West England's most powerful biomedical concentration outside the South East.

Such is the history, and such the opportunities. Two centuries of scientific and industrial revolution have created a huge educational, industrial and cultural infrastructure. And it still comes wrapped in romantic countryside.

vintage times for leisure

Felicity Goodey

'All intellectual improvement arises from leisure.' Samuel Johnson

The year 2002 will go down as a golden year for England's North West, not only as the year of the biggest sporting event ever staged in Britain – the Manchester Commonwealth Games – but also as the year when internationally renowned architects told Europe's biggest property fair that England's North West was a place reinventing itself through world-class design. A region which for too long had lived on past glories, and become perhaps too focused on what it still had to do to deal with the legacies of that great industrial era, suddenly saw itself through other people's eyes and found that, in reality, it had a whole new range of assets and attractions to celebrate.

Daniel Libeskind, architect of the visually striking Imperial War Museum North, gave an eloquent testimonial on the region's rising fortunes. "It's an area with open horizons, imagination, integrity and personal ambition merged together to give a fantastic aura which will be unique, not only in England, but I think in all of Europe," he observed.

The Libeskind building is on the Trafford side at the head of the Manchester Ship Canal, built in Victorian times to create the inland port of Manchester. On the opposite bank, in what is now Salford Quays, sits Michael Wilford's Lowry. This is a £120m international arts and entertainment complex; *The Times'* architectural critic Marcus Binney has described it as probably the most important piece of modern architecture in Britain today. Between the two they have won enough awards to fill the trophy cabinet at the world's most famous football club, Manchester United, whose hallowed turf is only a stone's throw away. And that is just one corner of one of the region's two great cities.

Winning the seventeenth Commonwealth Games threw a spotlight on the region. When the eyes of one billion people are focused on you, it is a powerful incentive to polish up the old and invest in the new. The North West has been a hive of activity over the past few years, and this was an opportunity to clean up large swathes of dereliction – the detritus of the industrial past. Anyone in search of dark satanic mills is now likely to be disappointed. Most have been swept away; a few remain in odd corners of the region, many now converted into museums, modern work space, or trendy apartments. East Manchester, once the home of traditional manufacturing, is being transformed into the site of a new sports city. First came the Velodrome, the national cycling centre, and already home to a number of international events. Is it a coincidence that Britain's current Olympic gold medal cycling champion Jason Queally comes from this region?

Centrepiece of the new developments is the £110m City of Manchester Stadium, built specially for the Games – another piece of highly-acclaimed modern design – and following the Games, the new home for Manchester City Football Club. All the new facilities have been designed not only to provide first class venues for the Games, but to encourage and support a growing market

Opposite If you fancy a trip on Europe's second highest roller-coaster, then head for Blackpool. Take your seat on The Big One and hold on tight as it lifts you 213ft above the Pleasure Beach, then hurtles back down at a speed of 74mph.

Right The strikingly designed Manchester Aquatics Centre is a new £32m swimming pool complex located in the heart of the city's education precinct. Largely funded by Sport England, it is the only complex in the UK with two 50-metre pools as well as separate diving and leisure pools.

Opposite Sport has become a major force for the regeneration of East Manchester with the 38,000-seat City of Manchester Stadium, a jewel in the crown of the XVII Commonwealth Games infrastructure. Substantially funded by the Sport England Lottery Fund, the stadium will become home to Manchester City FC when the 2002 Games are over.

in sport and sports tourism. The National Squash Centre, an International Tennis Centre and the Aqua Centre, with its elegant sculpted lines, are designed to meet the needs of everyone from championship competitors to the family wanting a bit of fun.

Is there a market? With household spending on attending sporting events 45 per cent higher than the UK average, the region is clearly sports mad. So it is not surprising that the quality of events on offer is world-class. The world's most famous steeplechase, the Grand National, draws 100,000 to Aintree, near Liverpool, every spring (and another near billion worldwide television audience); Test cricket is held on Lancashire's hallowed turf at Old Trafford each summer and there are dominant clubs in both rugby codes, especially League. There are also three golf courses with Open Championship pedigree, Royal Lytham and St Anne's, Royal Birkdale at Southport, and Royal Liverpool at Hoylake which is set to rejoin the other two as official Open venues after an absence of nearly 40 years.

Regionally, football is followed with religious passion. This is where the professional league was born in 1888 and from where it is still administered. Today it is home to several Premier League clubs including two of the world's most idolised – Liverpool and Manchester United. No wonder Preston North End's Deepdale Stadium complex is the location for the National Football Museum, fittingly housed under stands named after two of the sport's greatest legends – Sir Tom Finney and Bill Shankly – and honouring the original 'invincibles' of football. Preston's early dominance of the world's first league competition reflected Lancashire's leading role in the creation of prosperity, culture and leisure.

Opposite Trout Fishing at Ridgegate Reservoir, near Macclesfield. Angling is Britain's most popular participatory sport and the North West boasts some of the finest fishing.

Right Sailing on Budworth Mere, Cheshire. The North West has numerous stretches of open water, offering opportunities for a wide range of leisure activities.

The price of being the cradle of the industrial revolution was a decaying urban fabric, but over the past ten years the region has begun to see many of these physical liabilities as potential modern assets. From the Games site in east Manchester across the whole of the region, a clean up programme is reclaiming the extensive network of canals, warehouses and docks for tourism, housing and leisure.

Castlefield and Deansgate Locks in Manchester are two of many canal-side developments where once coal and cotton was unloaded for the mills. Today celebrity owned café bars like Barca and the Comedy Store are packed with revellers determined to party the night away. The IRA bomb which shattered Manchester's retail centre reawakened a desire once again to be a trend-setter, a world leader. Youth culture became the height of fashion as everyone from the city planners to the property developers, the music makers to the accountants and the lawyers, started a whirlwind of renewal. Thousands are flocking back to live in the city, mainly in designer loft apartments in converted warehouses. Some apartments now cost more than £1m. Gary Rhodes, Raymond Blanc and Nico opened restaurants to compete with home-grown talent like Paul Heathcote and some of the best Chinese and Indian restaurants in Europe. On the club scene they don't come any bigger than Cream in Liverpool.

The banking spine of Manchester, King Street, is now home to designer shops like Emporio Armani, where once only the starched collars of merchants and bankers presided; the Reform Club, no longer a gentleman's retreat, is now another trendy bar. The bankers and the lawyers did not go away, they moved to luxury office blocks next door to the Bridgewater Hall, Manchester's new International Concert Hall; the Royal Bank of Scotland's new headquarters will be in another designer complex called Spinningfields. New leisure and shopping complexes like the Great Northern, the Print Works and the Triangle have been created in refurbished and adapted Victorian buildings. Debates began as to whether Manchester could be a European style, 24 hour city. There is no debate any longer; Manchester is a city where you can dance, eat, drink, shop and party the night away and Liverpool is hard on its heels.

Victorian industrialists who amassed huge wealth displayed it in the great public buildings of the region's towns and cities. Neglected no more, these jewels are being restored and enhanced for the future. Once derelict warehouses which marred Liverpool's sublime waterfront are now home to the Tate and the fine Merseyside Maritime Museum at the Albert Dock. Liverpool's magnificent civic buildings have been restored and complemented by the new Conservation Centre, a major visitor attraction in its own right. Restored and refurbished, too, is the Walker, the 'National Gallery of the North', which houses one of

Above Granada Television's 'Coronation Street' has been with us for so long that it has been absorbed into the national psyche. For over 40 years, the previous night's episode of 'Corrie' has been discussed throughout the land, from the boardroom to the factory floor – quite an achievement for a programme centred around a single 'ordinary' street in Manchester.

Right Musicals, plays, concerts and ballets, the North West's theatres stage an almost endless variety of performances.

Europe's finest art collections. Just outside the city is the beautifully-restored Grade II nineteenth century Sefton Park Palm House, the resplendent home once again for exotic plants first brought back by the Victorian ship owners, merchants and industrialists who dominated world trade.

There is a new confidence about the two great cities and the graduates of many of the region's universities who used to believe that real opportunity and fun was only to be found in London, or further afield, are coming back to a region which now regularly hosts star names. West End musicals, like *Phantom of the Opera* and *Miss Saigon* play the Palace and the Opera House in Manchester and the Empire in Liverpool.

Star names like Tom Courtenay, Amanda Donohoe and Pete Postlethwaite are keen to play at the Royal Exchange, the free standing theatre-in-the-round built on the one acre floor of the former trading hall where world cotton prices were set. The Lowry has attracted the Paris Opera Ballet and the European premier of *Tantalus*. The MEN Arena hosts sell-out concerts for some of the biggest names in music, from Pavarotti to Bassey, Travis to Russell Watson. Sir Paul McCartney regularly returns to Liverpool, and Robbie Williams filled Old Trafford cricket ground and Daniel Barenboim the Bridgewater Hall.

Above The MEN Arena was the only UK location to receive a nomination for the International Venue of the Year Award, competing against other major venues such as the Sydney Entertainment Centre and the impressive Palais Omnisports in Paris. Each year the Arena plays host to a glittering succession of top performers from across the entire musical spectrum.

151

With three resident symphony orchestras the region's musical excellence reverberates across Europe and beyond. The Royal Liverpool Philharmonic Society, established in 1840, rejoices in its magnificent Art Deco concert hall, while the Hallé, founded in 1858 by Sir Charles Hallé, is now settled in the Bridgewater Hall, its new home, under the musical directorship of international conductor Mark Elder. The region has been coy about sharing some of these pleasures. At last some of the old family silver is being brought out, polished and re-presented. Rylands Library in Manchester and the Picton in Liverpool are among the finest libraries of the world, each based around a private collection created on the whim of one individual; Manchester has a breathtaking collection of Pre-Raphaelites. In the Lancashire town of Accrington the world's finest collection of Tiffany glass is to be found, shipped back by a local man who went to work for Tiffany in New York at the turn of the last century; for years it lay overlooked in packing cases. The paintings of LS Lowry are now rehoused at Salford Quays where they attract ten times as many people as before. St Helens has turned glass-making into an attraction, as has Stockport its hatting and Macclesfield its silk-making.

The region is blessed with other notable assets. It contains England's biggest lake (Windermere) and highest peak (Scafell Pike). It has one World Heritage Site (Hadrian's Wall) and three more likely to join the club. One of the National Trust's best-loved attractions, Beatrix Potter's house, is in the Lake District; Blackpool Pleasure Beach is Britain's biggest crowd-puller, and Chester Zoo has Britain's most visited wildlife attraction (having overtaken London Zoo in 2000). The biggest attraction of all, *Coronation Street*, still glues millions of viewers to their television sets each week, as it has for the past four decades.

Of the region's seven cities, Chester boasts mediaeval walls built on Roman foundations and its black and white Rows. Preston, at the heart of the royal Red Rose county of Lancashire, is the latest to be awarded city status, winning it in 2002 as part of the Queen's Golden Jubilee

Left One of Britain's unlikeliest international tourist attractions lies in a quiet North Lancashire market town. Against the odds, residents of Carnforth are restoring their railway station which was the location setting for one of the greatest romantic films, 'Brief Encounter', starring Celia Johnson and Trevor Howard. The popularity of director David Lean's masterpiece has barely faltered since he shot Noel Coward's play here in 1945.

Each year hundreds of Japanese and American film pilgrims worship at this cinematic shrine. Yet for 30 years the station lay derelict after its West Coast Main Line platforms closed, leaving only the unmanned junction platforms for Barrow and Yorkshire.

The handsome, cream-coloured sandstone station buildings of 1880 (designed by church architects Paley & Austin) narrowly escaped demolition. In an amazing display of people power, the Carnforth Station and Railway Trust, formed in 1996, have, with the help of grants, undertaken a magnificent £1m restoration of the station.

A room dedicated to Sir David Lean's work is planned with help from his widow Sandra. There will also be an authentic recreation of the refreshment room set from 'Brief Encounter', as well as restoration of the famous platform clock and a local heritage centre.

The station forecourt buildings once more create a fine visual and commercial focal point for Carnforth town centre. They are leased to Carnforth Connect, Britain's first Rural Intelligent Bus Service (RIBS), with the ticket office computer-linked to solar-powered village bus-stops for timetable enquiries.

celebrations. The Queen happens to be the Duke of Lancaster, yes the Duke, which tends to prompt the Duke of Edinburgh, when he is in the region and hears the loyal toast to, "Her Majesty, Duke of Lancaster", to quip, "and what does that make me then? The Duchess?"

A recent Mori poll found that the majority of outsiders, when asked what they most associated with England's North West, responded, 'countryside, and in particular the Lake District'. It is a mark of how blasé the indigenous population had become that this came as something of a surprise. The outsiders were right. But the Lake District National Park, along with the Peak Park and the Yorkshire Dales Park (part of which tumbles over into this region) are all so accessible that we sometimes forget how special they are.

Wordsworth and Tennyson were far more eloquent about the glories of the Cumbrian scenery than I could ever be. Foot and mouth did serious damage to the tourist trade, which has for many years been as important as farming to the Lake District. The experience has taught the business and agricultural community that tourism is a major part of the economy and should be professionally

Above The popular seaside resort of Blackpool is famous for its people-packed promenade and larger-than-life entertainment. Visitors flood to the resort all year round, be it for the fairground, the mixture of people and entertainment, or the illuminations.

grown and managed to provide a world-class range of products and experiences to delight the customer. Cumbrian food, as the locals have long known, is literally fit for a queen. Her Majesty's famous Herdwick lamb is now available to us all, along with many other regional delicacies.

Outside the formal national parks are vast tracts of rolling countryside in Lancashire and Cheshire. Stately homes abound and Cheshire has some of the finest gardens in the country. Most are now open to the public. The region still has a host of other treasures such as its private libraries and houses, which it has not yet decided to share. It may be of interest to the serious pleasure seekers that inhabitants of Alderley Edge are said to purchase more champagne per head of population than any other part of Britain!

The weather in the North West is often seen as a failing, although it is not as bad as popular folklore would imply – indeed, West Kirby in Merseyside is reputed to be the sunniest town in England – but there can be few regions which have consciously built quite as many weatherproof attractions as the North West. The most spectacular, perhaps, is on the outskirts of Manchester,

the Trafford Centre. This ornate pastiche of stately pleasure domes, is one of the largest out-of-town retail and leisure centres in Europe, where shopping has been turned into a weekend break. Here the climate is so controlled that the ceiling is painted like the sky and changes shade as the day waxes and wanes.

Tourism, leisure and culture now employ nearly ten per cent of the region's workforce. That is a powerful incentive to ensure that visitors like what they experience the first time and want to come back again. The region is beginning to grasp the opportunities; success is breeding success. Hotels are attracting new investment and quality operators, who in turn accelerate the improvements, bring new ideas and higher standards of customer service. Star names from sport and entertainment are happy to play here – and in many cases make the region their home. 2002 will have brought sport and entertainment to England's North West on a scale never seen before, and for a whole new generation of golden names, Manchester will forever be associated with the pinnacle of success.

Above Troutbeck in Windermere typifies everything that is good about the Lakes: tranquillity, rustic charm, a friendly welcome and vast swathes of unspoilt countryside. A perfect rural retreat, with room enough to accommodate a steady stream of visitors and enable them to lose each other and find peace and solitude.

Opposite What better venue for the stunning new National Football Museum than Preston, as Preston North End were first champions of the Football League.

Left De Vere Carden Park. Contrasting with the region's traditional seaside links, this Jack Nicklaus-designed golfers' paradise has 45 holes set in rolling Cheshire countryside. Carden Park, which also includes a luxury conference hotel, is home to an annual European Seniors Tour professional tournament.

Left below This idyllic cricketing scene, outside the village of Pott Shrigley, near Macclesfield, is repeated every weekend in the summer throughout the region.

157

From the Industrial Revolution to today's cultural revolution, the North West has been in the vanguard of change.

Opposite With its mock-Tudor Court House and manicured greens, it is hard to imagine that this is a key site of the Industrial Revolution. Yet, this is what Worsley is, for here, in 1761, the Duke of Bridgewater's canal was opened as the world's first purpose-built inland waterway. The Duke needed to carry coal cheaply from his local mines to Manchester and commissioned James Brindley to design a canal. The scheme was such a success that it heralded an explosion in canal building nationwide, allowing producers to transport their goods speedily and cheaply, encouraging the demand for goods that sparked the Industrial Revolution.

Left The Mathew Street Festival is held each summer in Liverpool and draws huge crowds, not only from the North West, but also from all around the world. It is just one example of the region's lively energy, which is reflected in a stream of constantly changing festivals and street entertainment.

Left below A fascinating tribute to Liverpool's 'Fab Four', the Beatles Story is a walk-through museum at the Albert Dock featuring audio-visual sets, original suits, personal items and letters, as well as recreations of the main places and events from their lives.

Above The renaissance of the North West is symbolised by Daniel Libeskind's stunning Imperial War Museum North at Trafford Park, Manchester.

ACKNOWLEDGEMENTS The Bluecoat Press wish to express their appreciation to Trevor Bates and Geoffrey Piper for their inspired contribution. The North West Business Leadership Team and the Northwest Development Agency would like to thank the very large number of people and organisations who have helped with the production of this book. Thousands of suggestions were received following a request for material during 2001. The only regret is that there is insufficient room in a publication of this kind to include all, or even most, of the many interesting features, achievements and attractions which have been suggested. We trust that the words and images which we have chosen fairly represent our region and adequately reflect the many expressions of enthusiasm we have received.